Frequently Asked Questions About Copyright

ISSUES AFFECTING THE U.S. GOVERNMENT

Prepared by
CENDI Copyright Working Group

Edited and updated by
Bonnie Klein
Defense Technical and Information Center
and
Gail Hodge
Information International Associates, Inc.

Published by
CENDI Secretariat
Information International Associates, Inc.
Oak Ridge, TN

October 8, 2008

Purpose and Use of this Document

This document is prepared by the CENDI Copyright Task Group in response to a request from the task group members and CENDI principals to address the issue of copyright from an operations perspective. In 1997, the CENDI Task Group identified a series of questions concerning copyright and intellectual property. These were documented as part of the Task Group's report, "Copyright and Intellectual Property: Operational Issues for CENDI Agencies." Realizing that it was not in a position to provide guidance for any particular agency, CENDI developed the concept of a Frequently Asked Questions document (FAQ) that could be used to educate librarians, information center staff, publications staff and agency authors about copyright.

The Copyright Law is complex and situation-based. Therefore, professional counsel for specific cases is advised. However, it is also hoped that this document will serve as a template for the development of agency Office of General Counsel approved documents that can provide more specific guidance for the individual agencies. It should be noted that this document primarily addresses U.S. Copyright Law as provided at Title 17 of the United States Code (17 USC – Copyrights) and Title 37 of the Code of Federal Regulations, Chapter II (37 CFR, Chapter II – Copyright Office, Library of Congress).

Copyright Notice

Notice of Change

The information presented in this FAQ is subject to changes enacted by U.S. Government policies, legislation and case law. *Direct comments about this document to* copyright@dtic.mil.

CENDI is an interagency cooperative organization composed of the scientific and technical information (STI) managers from the Departments of Agriculture, Commerce, Energy, Education, Defense, the Environmental Protection Agency, Health and Human Services, Interior, the National Aeronautics and Space Administration, the Government Printing Office, the National Archives and Records Administration, the National Science Foundation, and the Library of Congress. CENDI's mission is to help improve the productivity of federal science- and technology-based programs through the development and management of effective scientific and technical information support systems. In fulfilling its mission, CENDI member agencies play an important role in helping to strengthen U.S. competitiveness and address science- and technology-based national priorities.

SUMMARY OF CHANGES

CENDI/2008-1
CENDI Frequently Asked Questions about Copyright: Issues Affecting the U.S. Government

This revision, dated 8 October 2008--

- New version: October 2008 (*Old version: January 2002 (rev. August 2008)*)
- Adds section 5.3.7
- Updates References

TABLE OF CONTENTS

3.2.3   May the Government reproduce and disseminate U.S. Government works, such as journal articles or conference papers, which have been first published or disseminated by the private sector?

3.2.4   Can a U.S. Government work be reused after it has been published in a non-government product?

3.2.5   Many U.S. Government employees are under the impression that they must transfer copyright in works prepared as part of their job to the publisher of a journal or book in order to have an article published. Is this true?

3.2.6   Should U.S. Government employees sign publishing agreements for works produced as part of their official duties?

3.2.7   Is a work co-authored by a U.S. Government employee and a non-government employee copyrightable?

5.1.1   Does the U.S. Government have any special rights to use copyrighted material?

5.1.2   Are there any copyright issues related to the use of non-government abstracts or citations in U.S. Government authored bibliographies or databases?

5.1.3   Does copyrighted material lose its copyright status and protection if it becomes part of a U.S. Government work or is included in a compilation published by the Government?

5.1.4   May the U.S. Government use works of foreign governments or international organizations?

5.1.5   Can the Government translate a copyrighted work to which it does not hold copyright?

5.2.1   Are there any special policies that apply to Government libraries and archives?

5.2.2   Can digital material be copied for archival purposes? Can its format be changed?

5.2.3   What happens if the actual need for copyrighted material exceeds the exceptions granted in 17 USC § 107 and § 108?

5.2.4   Do copyright principles apply to materials purchased and licensed by Government libraries?

5.3.1   How can you determine if copyright permission is needed?

5.3.2   Is it necessary to get permission to use facts from a copyrighted source?

5.3.3   What should be considered when getting a license, release or permission?

5.3.4   Are there other rights that should be addressed when dealing with U.S. Government use of non-government works?

5.3.5   Can the Government transfer licenses or permission?

5.3.6   Must the Government request permission to include copyrighted material owned by a government employee in a U.S. Government work?

5.3.7   Does a government agency need a license to perform copyrighted music or show a copyrighted video at a government sponsored meeting or event?

5.4   Infringement by the Government

5.4.1   What acts constitute a copyright infringement?

5.4.2   Can a copyright owner sue the Government if the Government, or a contractor performing under a government contract, infringes the copyright?

5.4.3   What are the consequences for infringement by U.S. Government agencies or employees?

5.4.4   Who represents the government in copyright infringement suits?

6.0   APPLICABLE COPYRIGHT LEGISLATION AND OTHER RESOURCES ON THE INTERNET

BIBLIOGRAPHY

   U.S. Copyright Office Sources

   CONFU (Conference on Fair Use, 1994-98)

   Other Sources

   Websites (with copyright information)

   Websites (for copyright licensing and permissions)

   ListServs

Other Sources (from CENDI Copyright Task Group)

Government Agency Policies—A Sampling

Publisher Copyright Transfer Agreements—A Sampling

References

CENDI Copyright Task Group

CURRENT MEMBERS

Bill Adams (DOD/Army), Nancy Allard (NARA), Vicki Allums (DISA), Jane Barrow (DOD/Navy), James Bechtel (ONR), Dale Berkley (NIH), David Berthiaume (DoED), Gary Borda (NASA), JoAnne Calhoun (NASA), J. Chafin (HQDA), Chris Cole, Co-chair (NAL), Kathleen Coleman (EPA), Geoff Cooper (EPA), John Davenport (NARA), Dan Dzara (DOD/AF), Robin Edwards (NASA), Nancy Faget (GPO), Martha Fishel (NLM), Judy Gilmore (DOE/OSTI), Courtney Graham (NASA), Richard Gray (DOD/AF), Lynn Heimerl (NASA), Gail Hodge (CENDI), Michael Hoffman (DOE), Valerie Hurt (NIH), Sharon Jordan (DOE/OSTI), Robert Kasunic (LOC), James King (NRL), Flayo Kirk (DISA), Bonnie Klein, Co-chair (DTIC), Nancy Kremers (DARPA), Harry Lupuloff (DOD/AF), Neil Mark (USGS), Barbara McGarey (NIH), Hope O'Keeffe (LOC), Mary Rasenberger (LOC), John Raubitschek (DOD/Army), Janet Scheitle (GPO), Jerry Sheehan (NLM), Chris Weston (LOC)

PAST MEMBERS:

Barbara Bauldock (DOE/OSTI), Blaine Baker (DOD/AF), Nancy Collins (NTIS), Alice Cranor (DIA), Susan Cummings (NARA), Michelle Darcy (GPO), Dana Dobson (DoED), Caroline Early (NAL), Wally Finch (NTIS), Julia Giller (USGS), Jane Griffith (NLM), Kate Kase (USGS), Eve-Marie Lacroix (NLM), Richard Lambert (NIH), Mary Levering (LOC), Thomas McDonnell (ONR), Jan McNutt (DISA), R.L. Scott (DOE/OSTI), Jacqueline Streeks (NASA/CASI), Eric Vogel (NASA/CASI)

CENDI is an interagency cooperative organization composed of the scientific and technical information (STI) managers from the Departments of Agriculture, Commerce, Energy, Education, Defense, the Environmental Protection Agency, Health and Human Services, Interior, the National Aeronautics and Space Administration (NASA), the National Archives and Records Administration, the National Science Foundation and the Government Printing Office.

1.0   GLOSSARY OF TERMS

Author, under the U.S. Copyright Law, is either the person who actually creates a copyrightable work or, if the copyrightable work is created within the scope of employment, the employer of the person who actually creates the copyrightable work.

Berne Convention[1] is the Convention for the Protection of Literary and Artistic Works, signed at Berne, Switzerland, on September 9, 1886, and all acts, protocols, and revisions to these documents.

Clearance – see Permission

Collective work is a work, such as a periodical issue, anthology, or encyclopedia, in which a number of contributions, constituting separate and independent works in themselves, are assembled into a collective whole.

Compilation is a work formed by the collection and assembling of preexisting materials or of data that are selected, coordinated, or arranged in such a way that the resulting work as a whole constitutes an original work of authorship. The term "compilation" includes collective works.

Copyright refers to the exclusive rights granted to an author or owner of a copyrightable work. (See FAQ Section 2.1 and 17 USC § 106.[2])

Copyright Management Information (CMI) is defined under the Digital Millennium Copyright Act (DMCA)[3] as identifying information about a work, author, copyright owner, and in certain cases, the performer, writer or director of a work, as well as terms and conditions for use of the work, and such other information as the Register of Copyrights may prescribe by regulation. (See FAQ Section 2.4.6 and 17 USC § 1202(c).[4])

Copyright owner, with respect to any one of the exclusive rights comprised in a copyright, refers to the owner of that particular right. The exclusive rights provided by Copyright are completely divisible. Copyright in a work vests initially in the author or authors of the work. However, the author may assign some or all of his or her rights to another, e.g., to a publisher, if the work has appeared in a formal publication, who then becomes the owner of the rights assigned.

Derivative Work refers to a work that is based on, or modifies, one or more preexisting works. A copyright owner has the exclusive right to prepare or authorize the preparation of a derivative work based on the copyrighted work. If a derivative work, considered as a whole, represents an original work of authorship, it may be separately copyrightable. However, the copyright covers only original portions of the derivative work.

Fair Use is a statutory exception that allows the use of a copyrighted work for certain purposes without requiring permission. (See 17 USC § 107[5]).

Federal Acquisition Regulation (FAR)[6] was established to codify uniform policies for acquisition of supplies and services by executive agencies. It is issued and maintained jointly, pursuant to the OFPP Reauthorization Act, under the statutory authorities granted to the Secretary of Defense (DoD), Administrator of General Services (GSA) and the Administrator, National Aeronautics and Space Administration (NASA). The official FAR appears in the Code of Federal Regulations at 48 CFR Chapter 1.

First Sale Doctrine refers to the right of a buyer of a material object in which a copyrighted work is embodied to resell or transfer the object itself. Ownership of copyright is distinct from ownership of the material object. Section 109 of the Copyright Act permits the owner of a particular copy or phonorecord lawfully made under the Copyright Law to sell or otherwise dispose of possession of that copy or phonorecord without the authority of the copyright owner. Commonly referred to as the "first sale doctrine," this provision permits such activities as the sale of used books. The first sale doctrine is subject to limitations that permit a copyright owner to prevent the unauthorized commercial rental of computer programs and sound recordings. (See 17 USC § 202[7] and 17 USC § 109[8].)

Government Distribution or Dissemination means, in accordance with OMB Circular A-130,[9] Management of Federal Information Resources, the Government initiated distribution of information to the public. Dissemination within the meaning of the Circular does not include distribution limited to government employees or agency contractors or grantees, intra- or inter-agency use or sharing of government information, and responses to requests for agency records under the Freedom of Information Act (FOIA) (5 U.S.C. § 552[10]) or Privacy Act[11].

Government Publication is informational matter that is published as an individual document at Government expense or as required by law. (See Title 44 USC § 1901[12])

Government Records are all books, papers, maps, photographs, machine-readable materials, or other documentary materials, regardless of physical form or characteristics, made or received by an agency of the United States Government under federal law or in connection with the transaction of public business and preserved or appropriate for preservation by that agency or its legitimate successor as evidence of the organization, functions, policies, decisions, procedures, operations, or other activities of the Government or because of the informational value of the data in them. Library and museum material made or acquired and preserved solely for reference or exhibition purposes, extra copies of documents preserved only for convenience of reference, and stocks of publications and of processed documents are not included. (See 44 USC § 3301[13])

U.S. Government Work or a "work of the United States Government" is a work prepared by an officer or employee of the United States Government as part of that person's official duties. (See 17 USC § 101. Definitions[14]) In these FAQ's, the term "U.S. Government work" will be used to refer to a work of the United States Government and is distinct from works of state governments (See FAQ Section 3.1.3).

Intellectual Property refers to intangible property rights such as copyright, patents and trademarks that provide the owner with certain exclusive rights.

Joint Work is a work prepared by two or more authors with the intention that their contributions be merged into inseparable or interdependent parts of a unitary whole. (See 17 USC § 101.

Definitions[15]) The authors of a joint work are co-owners of copyright in the work. (See 17 USC § 201(a)[16])

License is a contractual agreement from a copyright owner or the owner's authorized agent, such as a third party vendor, allowing another party to exercise one or more of the exclusive rights provided the copyright owner under the Copyright Law (See FAQ Section 2.1.5). Licenses usually involve the payment of a fee or royalty. However, royalty free licenses are also legally possible; for example, see the National Library of Medicine *License Agreement for Use of the UMLS® Metathesaurus®*.[17]

Permission is an agreement from a copyright owner allowing another party to exercise one or more of the exclusive rights provided the copyright owner under the Copyright Law (See FAQ Section 2.1.5. Permission generally does not involve the transfer of any fees or reimbursements. Permission may also be referred to as a Copyright Release.

Publication is the distribution of copies or phonorecords of a work to the public by sale or other transfer of ownership or by rental, lease, or lending. The offering to distribute copies or phonorecords to a group of persons for purposes of further distribution, public performance, or public display, constitutes publication. A public performance or display of a work does not of itself constitute publication. (See 17 USC § 101. Definitions[18])

Transfer of copyright ownership is the act of transferring any or all of the exclusive rights comprised in a copyright from the copyright owner to another person or institution. Ownership is generally transferred through an assignment, mortgage, or exclusive license, whether or not it is limited in time or place of effect, but not including a nonexclusive license. (See 17 USC § 201(d)(2).[19]) Transfers must be in writing and must be signed by the party making the transfer. (See 17 USC § 204.[20])

2.0   COPYRIGHT BASICS

2.1   General Information Regarding Copyright

2.1.1   What is copyright?

Copyright is a form of protection provided by the laws of the United States (Title 17 of the United States Code (17 USC – Copyrights[21]) to the authors of original works of authorship including literary, dramatic, musical, artistic, and certain other intellectual works. (See also Title 37 Code of Federal Regulations (37 CFR, Chapter II[22]), which implements this statute.) Copyright protection arises automatically once an original work of authorship is fixed in a tangible medium of expression, now known or later developed; e.g., written, filmed, and recorded. It does not require that a copyright notice be placed on the work, that the work be published, or that the work be deposited or registered with the Copyright Office or any other body.

2.1.2   What is the history of copyright legislation in the U.S.?

The basis for Copyright Law comes from U.S. Constitution, Article 1, Section 8.[23]

"The Congress shall have power… to promote the Progress of Science and useful Arts, by securing for limited times to Authors and Inventors the exclusive right to their respective Writings and Discoveries."

The first federal Copyright Act enacted in 1790 was a codification of longstanding judicial doctrine. Since that date, Congress has periodically enacted major copyright revision bills modernizing the statute. The last copyright revision bill was enacted in 1976.

While most of the provisions of the current Copyright Law were contained in the Copyright Act of 1976, on a number of occasions Congress has amended that legislation to address new concerns. For example, in 1988 a number of changes were embraced to permit United States accession to the Berne Convention.[24] More recently, the copyright term was increased by the Sonny Bono Copyright Term Extension Act,[25] and issues relating to digital works were addressed in the Digital Millennium Copyright Act.[26] (See FAQ Section 2.4.6).

2.1.3   What works are eligible for copyright protection?

Copyright requires an original work of authorship to be fixed in a tangible medium of expression from which it can be perceived either directly or with the aid of a machine or device. Copyright protects the form of expression only and does not extend to the idea or concept underlying the work. (See FAQ Section 2.5, Other Forms of Intellectual Property Protection, for a discussion of the differences between copyright and other forms of intellectual property protection such as patents and trademarks.)

Categories of copyrightable works under Title 17 USC § 201 include: literary works such as educational materials and computer programs; musical works, including any accompanying words; dramatic works, including any accompanying music; pictorial, graphic and sculptural works; motion pictures and other audiovisual works; sound recordings; and architectural works. For U.S. Government works, see FAQ Section 3.

2.1.4   Can facts, databases and compilations be copyrighted?

Facts cannot be copyrighted. However, the creative selection, coordination and arrangement of information and materials forming a database or compilation may be protected by copyright. Note, however, that the copyright protection only extends to the creative aspect, not to the facts contained in the database or compilation.

2.1.5   What rights does copyright provide?

As stated in 17 USC § 106,[27] copyright gives the owner of the copyright the exclusive right to do and to authorize others to do the following:

- To reproduce the copyrighted work in copies or phonorecords;
- To prepare derivative works based upon the copyrighted work;

- To distribute copies or phonorecords of the copyrighted work to the public by sale or other transfer of ownership, or by rental, lease, or lending;
- To perform the copyrighted work publicly, in the case of literary, musical, dramatic, and choreographic works, pantomimes, motion pictures and other audiovisual works;
- To display the copyrighted work publicly, in the case of literary, musical, dramatic, and choreographic works, pantomimes, and pictorial, graphic, or sculptural works, including the individual images of a motion picture or other audiovisual work; and
- In the case of sound recordings, to perform the work publicly by means of a digital audio transmission.

In addition, certain authors of works of visual art have the rights of attribution and integrity described in 17 USC § 106A.[28] Limitations are outlined in FAQ Section 2.2.1.

For further discussion, see U.S. Copyright Office, Circular 101: Copyright Basics,[29] and Circular 40, Copyright Registration for Works of the Visual Arts.[30]

2.1.6 How long does copyright last?

Under current Copyright Law, the copyright term for works created by individuals on or after January 1, 1978, is the life of the author plus 70 years. For "works made for hire," the copyright term is 95 years from the date of first publication or 120 years from the date of its creation, whichever is earliest. The copyright term for works created before January 1, 1978, is a complicated determination and may require help from your General Counsel or the Copyright Office.

The current Copyright Law established dates at which Copyright protection for unpublished works expires and those works pass into the public domain. Unpublished works created prior to January 1, 1978, and not published, will pass into the public domain 70 years after the author's death or at the end of 2002, whichever is later. Unpublished works created prior to January 1, 1978, but which are published between then and the end of 2002, will pass into the public domain 70 years after the author's death or at the end of 2047, whichever is later. Additionally, all works published before 1923 are now in the public domain.

Publications that may help in this determination include:

The U.S. Copyright Law, Chapter 3 -- Duration of Copyright[31]

Information Circular 15a - Duration of Copyright: Provisions of the Law Dealing with the Length of Copyright Protection[32]

Fact sheet FL 15 - New Terms for Copyright Protection[33]

When Works Pass Into the Public Domain[34]

Copyright Term and the Public Domain in the United States[34a]

2.1.7 Is the copyright term extended or changed merely by copying the work to another medium; e.g., from print to CD-ROM?

No, the term of protection of a work is not affected by the fact that the owner has copied the work to another medium. If, in addition, new information is added, the new information if copyrightable could have its own term of protection.

2.2 Limitation on Copyright Protection

2.2.1 Are there any limitations to copyright protection?

Yes, 17 USC §§ 107 through 120[35] establish limitations or exceptions on these exclusive rights. One limitation is the doctrine of "fair use," which is set forth in 17 USC § 107.[36] (See FAQ Section 2.2.2 on Fair Use.) Other limitations include provisions for allowing compulsory licenses, use and copying by libraries, the sale of the work by the owner (See FAQ Section 1.0, Glossary, for definition of the "First Sale Doctrine") and uses which fall outside of the enumerated exclusive rights, such as performances that are not public.

2.2.2 What is "fair use"?

A fair use of a copyrighted work may include the practice of any of the exclusive rights provided by copyright, for example, reproduction for purposes such as criticism comment, news reporting, teaching (including multiple copies for classroom use), scholarship, or research. The "fair use" limitation found at 17 USC § 107,[37] is not defined in the statute and does not provide a bright line rule for determining what is or is not a fair use. Rather it identifies four factors that should be evaluated on a case-by-case basis in order to determine if a specific use is "fair". These factors, which should be considered together when determining fair use, are:

1) Purpose and character of the use, including whether such use is of a commercial nature or is for nonprofit educational purposes;
2) Nature of the copyrighted work;
3) Amount and substantiality of the portion used in relation to the copyrighted work as a whole; and
4) Effect of the use upon the potential market for or value of the copyrighted work.

The distinction between "fair use" and infringement can be unclear and is not easily defined. There is no right number of words, lines or notes that qualify as a fair use.

2.2.3 May the U.S. Government use the fair use exception?

Yes, the "fair use" exception applies to the U.S. Government. As with any other user, the use of copyrighted information by Government agencies and employees is assessed by the fair use factors to determine if the use is "fair" under 17 USC § 107. (See FAQ Section 5.1.1)

2.2.4 What is public domain?

Public domain refers to works that are not protected by copyright and are publicly available. They may be used by anyone, anywhere, anytime without permission, license or royalty payment.

A work may enter the public domain because the term of copyright protection has expired (see FAQ Section 2.1.6), because copyright has been abandoned, or in the U.S. because it is a U.S. Government work and there is no other statutory basis for the Government to restrict its access (see FAQ Section 3.1.5).

A work is not in the public domain simply because it does not have a copyright notice. Additionally, the fact that a privately created work is, with permission, included in a U.S. Government work does not place the private work into the public domain. The user is responsible for determining whether a work is in the public domain.

It is important to read the permissions and copyright notices on U.S. Government publications and Web sites. Many Government agencies follow the practice of providing notice for material that is copyrighted and not for those that are in the public domain. Examples of government agency copyright policies and statements are: National Library of Medicine,[38] NASA Center for AeroSpace Information (CASI),[39] and Library of Congress.[40]

2.2.5   Can a work that includes works in the public domain be copyrighted?

Yes. However, the copyright protects only the original contributions added by the author.

2.2.6   Does public release, disclosure or dissemination mean the same as public domain?

No, these terms are not synonymous and should not be used interchangeably. Public release, disclosure and dissemination describe the availability of a work. Publicly released, disclosed or disseminated information may be owned and protected by copyright, and therefore, not be in the public domain.

2.3   Ownership Of Copyright

2.3.1   Who can hold copyright?

Copyright ownership may be held by any person or institution. Typically, the author of a work owns the copyright in the work. However, under the U.S. Copyright Law, for a work made for hire, that is a work prepared by an employee within the scope of employment or a specially ordered or commissioned work, the employer or other person for whom the work was prepared is considered the author.

2.3.2   Can copyright be transferred from the author or owner to another party?

Yes, any and all of the copyright owner's exclusive rights may be transferred, but the transfer of exclusive rights is not valid unless that transfer is in writing and signed by the owner of the rights being transferred. (See 17 USC § 204[41]) Transfer of a right on a nonexclusive basis does not require a written agreement; however, you should check your Agency's policy.

No effective transfer of copyright can be made in the U.S. for U.S. Government works (see FAQ Section 3.0), because they are not eligible for copyright protection under the U.S. Copyright Law.

2.3.3 How can the owner of a copyrighted work be identified?

If you want to contact the copyright owner regarding use of a copyrighted work, the best place to start is with the work itself. Copyright notices in published works identify the owner at the time the work was published. However, copyright ownership may have changed since publication. The copyright notice and any permissions are often printed on the back of the title page in books. Most owners will be apparent, particularly for relatively current works. However, identifying the specific owner may be more difficult for journal articles, gray literature and older works. Affiliation of the author may suggest ownership or may help to locate the individual author, but is not in itself definitive. The U.S. Copyright Office provides some suggestions in Copyright Office Circular 22.[42]

Additionally, Copyright Office records, including registration information and recorded documents, are available through LOCIS (Library of Congress Information System[43]), or a newer web-based search system. Information, including ownership information, is available for works registered for copyright since January 1, 1978. The information may be searched online by title of the work, author and copyright claimant.

2.4 Copyright and the Internet

2.4.1 Does the Copyright Law apply to materials on the Internet or the Web?

Yes, the Internet is another form of publishing or disseminating information; therefore, copyright applies to Web sites, e-mail messages, Web-based music, etc. Simply because the Internet provides easy access to the information does not mean that the information is in the public domain or is available without limitations. Copyrighted works found on the Internet should be treated the same as copyrighted works found in other media.

2.4.2 Can the published version of a U.S. Government work that has been published in a non-government product be posted on a public Web site?

It depends. If the publisher has made original and creative contributions to the published work, the publisher may have some rights. Check with your General Counsel's Office or agency policy. Alternatively, the original manuscript as submitted to the publisher could be posted. (See FAQ Sections 3.2.3 and 3.2.4.)

2.4.3 Does fair use apply to the Internet?

Yes, fair use applies to materials and use of works found or placed on the Internet. The same factors will be considered as for fair use in print (see FAQ Section 2.2.2).

2.4.4 How can I determine what uses can be made of materials found on the Internet?

As in the print environment, it is not necessary for an author to include a copyright statement on the material in order for the work to maintain its copyright protection. However, you may find notices on the home page or on special terms and condition pages that provide for specific uses.

2.4.5 Are copyright notices required on materials on Government Web sites?

It is good practice to provide notice whenever possible, even though it is not required. In addition, there may be disclaimers and use notices that apply to use of the material. Check your Agency policy regarding Web site notices. For further discussion, see the CENDI Whitepaper Don't Keep the Public Guessing: Best Practices in Notice of Copyright and Terms & Conditions of Use for Government Website Content (CENDI/04-4). Also see examples listed in Section 6.0.

2.4.6 Is it a copyright infringement to link from your website to copyrighted material on another?

No. In April, 2000, Federal Judge Harry L. Hupp in his ruling on deep linking in *Ticketmaster vs. Tickets.com, Inc.,* 2000 U.S. Dist. LEXIS 12987 (D. Cal. 2000) states that, "...hyperlinking does not itself involve a violation of the Copyright Act (whatever it may do for other claims) since no copying is involved." Many organizations encourage links by posting terms and conditions and how-to instructions on their websites, usually under the headings of Copyright, Legal Notices, or About Us. For examples, see the *Washington Post*[44] and the *New York Times*.[45] However, be aware of "other claims" and court rulings which prohibit framing, misuse of trademarks, bypassing advertising, etc.

2.4.7 Does the Digital Millennium Copyright Act (DMCA) of 1998 expand protection of works on the Internet?

Yes, the DMCA (Pub. L. No. 105-304, 112 Stat. 2860[46]) added Chapter 12 to the U.S. Copyright Law.[47] The DMCA prohibits any person from circumventing a technological measure that effectively controls access to a work protected under the U.S. Copyright Act, 17 U.S.C. § 1201(a)(1)[48]. The Copyright Office will determine whether any classes of works should be subject to exemptions for the prohibitions and will publish lists of such exempt classes. The DMCA also makes it illegal for a person to manufacture, import, offer to the public, provide or otherwise traffic in any technology, product, service, device, component or part thereof which is primarily designed or produced to circumvent a technological measure that effectively controls access to or unauthorized copying of a work protected by copyright, has only a limited commercially significant purpose or use other than circumvention of such measures, or is marketed for use in circumventing such measures, 17 U.S.C. § 1201(a)(2)[49].

In addition the DMCA prohibits, among other actions, the intentional removal or alteration of copyright management information and the knowing addition of false copyright management information if these acts are done with intent to induce, enable, facilitate or conceal a copyright infringement, 17 U.S.C. § 1202[50]. Each prohibition is subject to a number of statutory exceptions.

The DMCA also provides certain limitations on service provider liability with respect to information residing, at direction of a user, on a system or network that the service provider controls or operates, 17 U.S.C. § 512[51]. However, this "safe harbor" provision may not be necessary for Government agencies qualifying as service providers because they are not liable for contributory copyright infringement (see FAQ Section 5.1.5).

Further, the DMCA creates an exemption for making a copy of a computer program by activating a computer for purposes of maintenance or repair. For further discussion, see the U.S. Copyright Office Summary of the DMCA.[52]

2.5   Other Forms O\of Intellectual Property Protection

2.5.1   Are there other forms of intellectual property protection?

Yes, there are other forms of intellectual property protection including patents and trademarks. Copyright differs from patents and trademarks in both the terms and kind of coverage that is granted. Copyright protects original works of authorship such as literary works, phonorecords, dramatic works, etc. Patents[53] protect new, useful and non-obvious inventions such as processes, machines, manufactures and compositions of matter. Trademarks[54] protect words, phrases, symbols or designs, such as logos or names of products or organizations, that identify and distinguish the source of goods or services of one party from those of another. Each type of intellectual property differs in the subject matter and requirements for protection, the length of time that the protection holds, how it can be transferred, the basis and penalties incurred for infringement of the exclusive rights provided, and the kind of exemptions that are allowed. For more information, contact the U.S. Patent and Trademark Office.[55]

3.0   U.S. GOVERNMENT WORKS

3.1   Government Works

3.1.1   What is a U.S. Government work?

A "work of the United States Government," referred to in this document as a U.S. Government work, is a work prepared by an officer or employee of the United States Government as part of that person's official duties. (See 17 USC § 101, Definitions.[56])

Contractors, grantees and certain categories of people who work with the government are not considered government employees for purposes of copyright. Also not all government publications and government records are government works (See FAQ Section 1.0, Definitions).

An officer's or employee's official duties are the duties assigned to the individual as a result of employment. Generally, official duties would be described in a position description and include other incidental duties. Official duties do not include work done at a government officer's or employee's own volition, even if the subject matter is government work, so long as the work was not required as part of the individual's official duty. (S.REP. NO. 473, 94th Cong., 2d Sess. 56-57) (1976) "A government official or employee should not be prevented from securing copyright in a work written at his own volition and outside his duties, even though the subject matter involves his government work or his professional field.") For further discussion, see Tresansky, John O. *Copyright in Government Employee Authored Works*.[57] 30 Cath. L. Rev. 605 (1981).

The following cases give examples of some related issues:

Public Affairs Associates v. Rickover,[58] 284 F.2d 262, 268 n.20 (D.C. Cir. 1960), vacated on other grounds for insufficient record, 369 U.S. 111 (1962)

Herbert. v. United States, 36 Fed. Cl. 299 (Fed. Cl. 1996). The court said: "The specific task need not be individually assigned in order to qualify as part of the official functions of a government employee. Where a government employee's official functions include research, generally, the employee may lose the right to sue for copyright infringement even where he was not specifically required to perform the work at issue."

3.1.2 Is a U.S. Government work provided copyright protection?

In the United States, U.S. Government works are covered by 17 USC § 105.[59] "Copyright protection … is not available for any work of the United States Government, but the United States is not precluded from receiving and holding copyrights transferred to it by assignment, bequest, or otherwise." Exceptions are available for certain works of the National Institute for Standards and Technology (NIST) and the U.S. Postal Service. Copyright protection may be available for U.S. Government works outside the United States (see FAQ Section 3.1.6). When a copyrighted work is transferred to the U.S. Government, the Government becomes the copyright owner and the work retains its copyright protection.

3.1.3 Does 17 USC §105[60] apply to works of state and local governments?

No, it applies only to federal government works. State and local governments may and often do claim copyright in their publications. It is their prerogative to set policies that may allow, require, restrict or prohibit claim of copyright on some or all works produced by their government units.

3.1.4 What is the history of the copyright treatment of U.S. Government works?

Ever since 1895, statutory provisions have prohibited the assertion of copyright in any publication of the U.S. Government. The provisions have been only slightly modified since their enactment. See *"Copyright in Government Publications: Historical Background, Judicial Interpretation, and Legislative Clarification." CPT Brian R. Price. Military Law Review. Vol. 74. (1976), p. 19-63.*

3.1.5 Since U.S. Government works are not protected by copyright in the U.S., are all U.S. Government works publicly available without restriction in the U.S.?

No. The fact that U.S. Government works are not protected under the U.S. Copyright Law does not create a requirement that all U.S. Government works be made publicly available without restriction (See Gellman, Robert M. Twin Evils: Government Copyright and Copyright-like

Controls Over Government Information.[61] Syracuse Law Review, 999, 1995. ADA394923). See Pfeiffer v. Central Intelligence Agency[62], 60 F.3d 861 (D.C. Cir. 1995). Federal laws and agency policies govern the public release of U.S. Government information. Examples include Executive Order 13292, Classified National Security Information, OMB Circular A-130,[63] Management of Federal Information Resources, Department of Defense Directive 5230.9 Clearance of DoD Information for Public Release[64], April 9, 1996, ASD (PA) and DOD Instruction 5230.29 Security and Policy Review of DoD Information for Public Release.[65] However, while the Government is not required to publicly disseminate all U.S. Government works, the Government does not restrict the use or distribution of most categories of U.S. Government works.

Despite the general policy of free and open information dissemination, there are exceptions based on a number of factors. Certain statutes (see Freedom of Information Act (FOIA) Exemptions[66]) provide the Government with authority to restrict access to U.S. Government works, for example, for purposes of national security, export control, and the filing of patent applications. U.S. Government works should undergo appropriate security, export control and policy reviews by the releasing agency before being cleared for public availability. Additionally, for the purposes of specific agreements, such as Cooperative Research and Development Agreements (CRADA's[67]) and NASA Space Act Agreements[68], the Government has statutory authority to withhold from public dissemination, including dissemination under FOIA, certain Government produced information for a specified period of time.

Some agencies may have additional statutory authority to impose conditions for use. Reasons include ensuring that copyrighted information contained in the government product is recognized, adhering to agreements with other parties, and maintaining contact with users to ensure maintenance and updating of critical information. For example, see NLM's Terms and Conditions for the Visible Human Project[69] and the License Agreement for Use of the UMLS® Metathesaurus®.[70] Issues related to joint authorship or sponsorship with non-government authors or organizations may also arise.

3.1.6 If an item has a GPO number (#) or an Agency number (#), can I assume it is not copyrighted?

No, not all Government Printing Office or Government agency publications are U.S. Government works. For example, Government Printing Office publications and Agency publications may include works copyrighted by a contractor or grantee; copyrighted material assigned to the U.S. Government; or copyrighted information from other sources.

3.1.7 Does the Government have copyright protection in U.S. Government works in other countries?

Yes, the copyright exclusion for works of the U.S. Government is not intended to have any impact on protection of these works abroad (S. REP. NO. 473, 94th Cong., 2d Sess. 56 (1976)). Therefore, the U.S. Government may obtain protection in other countries depending on the treatment of government works by the national copyright law of the particular country. Copyright is sometimes asserted by U.S. Government agencies outside the United States.

3.1.8 Is the Government required to provide notice that there is no U.S. copyright on its works?

No, but while such a notice is not required, it is helpful to potential users of the material to identify any rights the Government may or may not have in the work. Agencies may have policies about providing notice. For more information, consult your General Counsel.

A good example of a notice is:

> This is a work of the U.S. Government and is not subject to copyright protection in the United States. Foreign copyrights may apply.

To avoid confusion in situations where Government works are included in compilations with non-government material, the Government should put notices on every copyrighted item included in a U.S. Government work. Documentation related to permissions granted to the Government for use of such works should be retained.

3.1.9 Are Government websites provided copyright protection?

In accordance with 17 USC §105[71], works prepared by government employees as part of their official duties are not subject to copyright protection in the U.S. (See FAQ Sections 3.1.1 and 3.1.2). This applies to government employee prepared works posted to government websites and to the government website itself if government employees as part of their official duties prepare it.

However, if a government website is developed or maintained by a contractor, parts of the website authored by the contractor that are subject to copyright protection (i.e., that qualify as copyrightable subject matter) are protected by copyright. Ownership of the copyright and the respective rights of the Government and the contractor are in accordance with the terms of the contract under which the web site was developed or maintained. Additionally, it is possible that copyrighted works owned by others may be posted to government websites. Copyrighted works that are not owned by the Government should be included on government websites only with permission of the copyright owner and should include an appropriate copyright notice.

3.2 U.S. Government Works Included in Non-Government Works

3.2.1 May another publisher or individual republish a U.S. Government work and assert copyright?

A publisher or individual can republish a U.S. Government work, but the publisher or individual cannot legally assert copyright unless the publisher or individual has added original, copyright protected material. In such a case, copyright protection extends only to the original material that has been added by the publisher or individual. (See 17 USC § 403[72] regarding copyright notice requirements for works incorporating U.S. Government works.)

3.2.2 Can a U.S. Government work be copyrighted if it is included in conference proceedings with other works that are copyrighted?

No, a U.S. Government work is not protected by copyright in the U.S (see FAQ Section 3.1.2). However, other works in the proceedings may be copyrighted (see FAQ Section 2.1.4). Additionally, the creative aspect of the compilation of materials, e.g., selection, coordination or arrangement, may be protected by copyright.

3.2.3 May the Government reproduce and disseminate U.S. Government works, such as journal articles or conference papers, which have been first published or disseminated by the private sector?

Assuming the article is written by a government employee as part of his or her official duties and the publisher does not add original, copyright protected content, then the government may reproduce and disseminate an exact copy of the published work either in paper or digital form. (Matthew Bender & Co. v. West Publishing Co.,[73] 158 F.3d 674 (2d Cir. 1998), cert. denied, 119 S. Ct. 2039 (1999)).

3.2.4 Can a U.S. Government work be reused after it has been published in a non-government product?

Yes, U.S. Government works as originally submitted to the publisher (e.g., manuscripts, charts, photographs, etc.) may be reused in another publication.

3.2.5 Many U.S. Government employees are under the impression that they must transfer copyright in works prepared as part of their job to the publisher of a journal or book in order to have an article published. Is this true?

No, a paper, report, or other work prepared by an employee of the U.S. Government as part of that person's official duties is a U.S. Government work. Copyright protection is not provided for U.S. Government works under U.S. Copyright Law. Therefore, there is no U.S. Copyright to be transferred. U.S Government employees should inform the publisher of their employment status and should not sign any document purporting to transfer a U.S. copyright as a prerequisite to publication.

Additionally, a U.S. Government work may be protected under foreign copyright laws. The law of the foreign country governs ownership of foreign copyrights in U.S. Government works. The owner of the copyright may license or transfer a foreign copyright. The transfer of a foreign copyright owned by the U.S. Government must be executed by an authorized official of the Agency, who is almost never the U.S. Government author.

3.2.6 Should U.S. Government employees sign publishing agreements on works produced as part of their official duties?

Many publishers have standard forms that provide a specific space for authors to indicate that they are U.S. Government employees or that they are working on the Government's behalf. For examples, see the IEEE Copyright Form[74] and the Kluwer Academic/Plenum Publishing Transfer of Copyright Form[75].

However, many publishing agreements include other terms, such as indemnification or choice of law that the government employee may not have authority to accept. Employees should seek approval from their own organizations before signing such agreements.

The following is an example of wording for a permission form from the National Library of Medicine that can be suggested to a publisher.

> The U.S. Copyright Act provides that federal government employees cannot copyright material prepared in the course of their employment. As an employee of the [name department or agency], I have no copyright interest to assign, and upon the recommendation of the Office of General Counsel, [acronym for department or agency], must decline to sign the copyright assignment.
>
> Although for the above reasons I am technically unable to assign any copyright to [name publication], I still request and authorize you to publish the submitted article in accordance with your standard editorial policies. I hope this letter will be sufficient authorization for your needs to enable you to consider it favorably.

3.2.7 Is a work co-authored by a U.S. Government employee and a non-government author copyrightable?

A "joint work" is a work prepared by two or more authors with the intention that their contributions be merged into inseparable or interdependent parts of a unitary whole (see 17 USC § 101.[76]). The authors of a joint work are co-owners of the copyright in the work, unless there is an agreement to the contrary (see 17 USC § 201.[77]).

If a joint work is interdependent, contributions are generally created independently by separate co-authors with the intention to merge them into a unitary whole, and therefore they comprise separable parts. One should be able to isolate the contributions of a government employee from the contributions of a non-government employee. If, on the other hand, co-authors collaborated on much or all of a joint work, it will be considered inseparable, and it may be impossible to determine where the contributions of one author end and the other author or authors begin. Therefore, for an inseparable joint work, it is difficult or impossible to isolate the contribution of government employees from contributions of non-government employees. When the U.S. Government is joint author with a non-government entity, the law on how much of the work is protected by copyright is unsettled and is thus open to differing interpretations. In such situations, you should consult your Office of General Counsel.

Moreover, while the Copyright law provides that authors of a joint work are co-owners of the work, the law regarding how much the Government, as a joint author, may own is unsettled and thus open to differing interpretations. The notes following section 201 of the Copyright Act (17 U.S.C §201) state that, "Under the bill, as under current law, co-owners of a copyright would be treated generally as tenants in common, with each co-owner having an independent right to use or license the use of a work, subject to a duty of accounting to the other for any profits." Nonetheless, to protect the Government's interests, it would be prudent to obtain a license from the non-government co-owner to use and distribute the work.

Since joint authorship is a collaboration in which the authors have the intent from the beginning to create an integrated work, when it is anticipated that a government employee will participate as a joint author of a work arising under a contract or assistant agreement, it is advisable to consult your General Counsel and the outside author concerning the unsettled nature of the law.

4.0 WORKS CREATED UNDER A FEDERAL GOVERNMENT CONTRACT OR GRANT

4.1 If a work was created under a Government contract, who holds the copyright?

Unlike works of the U.S. Government, works produced by contractors under government contracts are protected under U.S. Copyright Law. (See Schnapper v. Foley, 667 F.2d 102 (D.C. Cir. 1981), cert. denied, 455 U.S. 948 (1982).) The ownership of the copyright depends on the terms of the contract. Contract terms and conditions vary between civilian agencies or NASA and the military.

Civilian agencies and NASA are guided by the Federal Acquisition Regulations (FAR)[78]. There are a number of FAR provisions that can affect the ownership of the copyright (see also FAQ Section 4.2 on data rights in SBIR contracts and Section 4.6 on the data rights for special works). FAR Subpart 27.4—Rights in Data and Copyrights[79]<74> provides copyright guidance for the civilian agencies and NASA. In addition, Agencies may have their own FAR Supplements that should be followed.

Under the FAR general data rights clause (FAR 52.227-14)[80], except for works in which the contractor asserts claim to copyright, the Government has unlimited rights in all data first produced in the performance of a contract and all data delivered under a contract unless provided otherwise in the contract. Unless provided otherwise by an Agency FAR Supplement, a contractor may, without prior approval of the Contracting Officer, assert claim to copyright in scientific and technical articles based on or containing data first produced in the performance of a contract and published in academic, technical or professional journals, symposia proceedings, or the like. The express written permission of the Contracting Officer is required before the contractor may assert or enforce the copyright in all other works first produced in the performance of a contract. However, if a contract includes Alternate IV of the clause, the Contracting Officer's approval is not required to assert claim to copyright. Whenever the contractor asserts claim to copyright in works other than computer software, the Government, and others acting on its behalf, are granted a license to reproduce, prepare derivative works, distribute, perform and display the copyrighted work. For computer software the scope of the Government's license does not include the right to distribute to the public (see FAQ Section 4.3).

Occasionally there may be a special provision outside the FAR clauses that addresses data rights (this would also cover databases), but such provisions would have to be included in the contract, statement of work or other agreement that is in place. The specific language should be discussed with the Contracting Officer.

The Department of Defense (DoD) is guided by the Defense Federal Acquisition Regulation

Supplement (DFARS) Subpart 227.71 – Rights in Technical Data[81] and Part 211[82] and Part 252[83] provisions that affect the ownership of copyright for works created under contract. DFARS Subpart 227.72[84] provides the copyright guidance for DoD (FAR 27.400[85]). The DFARS recognizes that the contractor owns the copyright for works created under contract (DFARS 227.7103-9[86], DFARS 252.227-7013-4[87]). If a special clause is inserted into a contract (DFARS 252.227-7020[88]), the contractor must assign the copyright to the Government.

While the Government has rights in more than just deliverables, as a practical matter the Government may have difficulty getting access to data unless it is either a deliverable or the contractor publishes it with a notice acknowledging the Government's sponsorship. The FAR requires an acknowledgment of Government sponsorship for contractor publications (see FAQ Sections 4.3 and 4.8). However, the DFARS does not. Therefore, it is advisable that works in which the Government desires rights are identified in the contract as deliverables. For software applications, the contract terms and conditions should also specify the format for delivery. If the Government needs to maintain or further develop the software program, it should consider expressly requiring delivery of source code.

4.2 Are data rights any different under special programs such as the Small Business Innovative Research (SBIR) Program?

Yes. In some cases, the particular program, such as the SBIR program, includes special copyright provisions. The FAR SBIR data rights clause, 52.227-20[89] permits an SBIR contractor to assert copyright ownership unless there is specific language in the contract to the contrary. If claim to copyright is made, the Government gets the same license as it receives under the FAR general data rights clause, 52.227-11 (see FAQ Section 4.3). Additional restrictions on the Governments use of SBIR Data may apply. SBIR data is data first produced by an SBIR contractor in the performance of an SBIR contract that is not generally known and that is not already available to the Government or has not been made available to others without an obligation of confidentiality. If SBIR Data delivered to the Government is marked with the SBIR Rights Notice provided in the clause, the Government may use the data for government purposes only, and cannot disclose the data outside the Government (except for use by support contractors) for a specified period of time. This additional restriction is intended to provide incentives for the development or commercialization of the technology or product by the private partner.

4.3 If the contractor is allowed to assert copyright in a work produced under a Government contract, what rights does the Government have?

A contractor's assertion of copyright in a work produced under a DFARS contract does not provide any restrictions to the Government's use of the work (see DFARS 227.7103-9[90] and 227.7203-9[91]). In a FAR contract, if the contractor is permitted to assert copyright, the Government will acquire a license to the copyrighted work. The extent of the license may depend on the type of work created (see FAR 52.227-14[92]).

Under the FAR, when a contractor asserts copyright in a work first produced in the performance of a contract with a civilian agency or NASA, the contractor must place a copyright notice acknowledging the government sponsorship (including contract number) on the work when it is delivered to the Government, as well as when it is published or deposited for registration with the U.S. Copyright Office (see FAQ Section 4.8). If no copyright notice is placed on the work, the Government obtains unlimited rights in the work. Unlimited rights allow the Government to provide the work to another contractor and distribute the work to the public, including posting the work to a public web site. Otherwise, when claim to copyright is made the Contractor grants the Government, and others acting on its behalf, a license to the work.

The Government's license is a nonexclusive, irrevocable, worldwide license to use, modify, reproduce, release, perform, display or disclose the work by or on behalf of the Government. The Government may use the work within the Government without restriction, and may release or disclose the work outside the Government and authorize persons to whom release or disclosure has been made to use, modify, reproduce, release, perform, display, or disclose the work on behalf of the government. The Government's license includes the right to distribute copies of the work to the public for government purpose. While the contractor may assign its copyright in "scientific and technical articles based on or containing data first produced in the performance of a contract" to a publisher, the Government's license rights attach to the articles upon creation and later assignment by the contractor to a publisher are subject to these rights. Under some FAR data rights clauses, if the work is a computer program, the right to release or disclose the computer program to the public is not included in the Government's license. If there is any question as to the scope of the Government's license, the Contracting Officer or your General Counsel should be consulted.

An example of a copyright statement, which includes a government license, for use with works created under contracts with civilian agencies and NASA is:

> COPYRIGHT STATUS: This work, authored by _____ employees, was funded in whole or in part by _____ under U.S. Government contract _____, and is, therefore, subject to the following license: The Government is granted for itself and others acting on its behalf a paid-up, nonexclusive, irrevocable worldwide license in this work to reproduce, prepare derivative works, distribute copies to the public, and perform publicly and display publicly, by or on behalf of the Government. All other rights are reserved by the copyright owner.

4.4 Does the Government have the same rights to use copyrighted material produced outside of a Government contract but included in a work produced under a Government contract as it does to portions of the work first produced in performance of the contract?

It depends. Under both the FAR and the DFARS, the contractor may not include copyrighted material in the work created for the Government without identifying the copyrighted material to the Contracting Officer and obtaining the Contracting Officer's permission to incorporate the copyrighted material. Normally, the contractor provides a license to the copyrighted material equivalent to the license set forth in the contract. However, the contracting officer may approve a license of more limited scope if appropriate (see FAR 27.404(f)(2)[93] and DFARS 227.7103-9(a)(2)[94]).

4.5 May a Government contractor voluntarily transfer its copyright to the Government?

Yes. The Government is not precluded from receiving and holding copyrights transferred to it by assignment. (See 17 USC § 105.) A Copyright assigned or otherwise transferred to the Government does not lose its copyright status or protection. The Government may record transfers of copyright with the U.S. Copyright Office and may register copyrights transferred to it.

4.6 Can a contractor be forced to transfer its copyright to the Government?

Yes. Under the FAR special works data rights clause, 52.227-17[95], in addition to requiring the Contracting Officer's written permission before a contractor may assert copyright ownership in material first produced under the contract, the Contracting Officer may instead direct the contractor to assign the copyright to the Government. Additionally, in accordance with FAR Section 27.404 (g)(3)[96], agencies may, to the extent provided in their FAR supplements, place limitations or restrictions on the contractor's right to use, release to others, reproduce, distribute, or publish any data first produced in the performance of the contract, including a requirement to assign copyright to the Government. Thus, Agency FAR supplements (e.g., the NASA FAR Supplement at 1852.227-14[97]) may also direct contractors in this way.

DFARS clause 252.227-7020[98] automatically directs the contractor to assign the copyright to the Government.

4.7 May a contractor use works it produced under a Government contract?

Yes, in most cases a contractor may use works it produced under a government contract. However, depending on the data rights clause in the contract, restrictions may apply. Under the FAR general data rights clause, 52.227-14,[99] the contractor must obtain authorization from the Contracting Officer to assert claim to copyright in a work created under the contract or no copyright may be asserted (see FAQ Section 4.1). However, in either situation, the contractor shall have the right to use, release to others, reproduce, distribute, or publish any data first produced or specifically used by the contractor in the performance of the contract, except to the extent such data may be subject to the federal export control or national security laws or regulations, may include restrictive markings or notices, or unless otherwise set forth in the contract (see FAR 27.404(g)[100] and 52.227-14(d)[101]). Agency FAR supplements may include more restrictive terms including the right to require the contractor to assign the copyright to the Government.

Under the FAR special works data rights clause 52.227-17,[102] the contractor shall not use any work first produced in the performance of the contract for purposes other than the performance of the contract, nor shall the contractor release, reproduce, distribute, or publish any such work, nor authorize others to do so, without written permission of the Contracting Officer.

Likewise, DFARS clause 252.227-7013[103] recognizes the contractor's copyright, while DFARS clause 252.227-7020[104] directs the contractor to assign the copyright to the Government. However, DFARS 227.7106(b)[105] notes that a contractor "retains use and disclosure rights" even after such an assignment. Therefore, the Government must negotiate a special license if it wishes to restrict a contractor's use of works it produced under contract. There may be other restrictions to the contractor's use, such as export control, national security, etc.

4.8 Must a contractor place a copyright notice or acknowledgement of the Government's rights and sponsorship on a work produced under Government contract?

Yes, the FAR requires that any contractor claiming copyright ownership to material first produced under a FAR contract affix the copyright notice and acknowledgement of government sponsorship (including the contract number) on all copies delivered to the Government, on all published copies, and on all copies deposited with the U.S. Copyright Office (See FAR 27.404(f)(1)(v)[106]), although the Copyright Law has no copyright notice requirement for works created on or after March 1, 1989. If these notices are not affixed, the Government has unlimited rights. See FAQ Section 4.3 for an example of a copyright statement for use with works created under civilian agency and NASA contracts.

Under the DFARS, a copyright notice is not required. (See DFARS 252.227-7013(f) and 252.227-7014(f)[107])

4.9 What are the rules regarding works produced under Government grants and cooperative agreements?

The data rights clauses in grants and cooperative agreements are flexible but generally allow the recipient to assert copyright. For works created under grants and cooperative agreements with colleges, universities, hospitals and non-profit organizations, all federal agencies adhere to the policies of OMB Circular A-110 [108] Uniform Administrative Requirements for Grants and Agreements With Institutions of Higher Education, Hospitals, and Other Non-Profit Organizations and to OMB Circular A-102,[109] Grants and Cooperative Agreements with State and Local Governments when the grantee is a state or local agency such as a state university. Section 36 of Circular A-110[110] provides that a grantee may assert copyright in any work that was developed under the grant or cooperative agreement. The Federal awarding agency reserves a royalty-free, nonexclusive and irrevocable right to reproduce, publish, or otherwise use the work for federal purposes, and to authorize others to do so. It should be noted that new requirements for providing government access[111] to information created from grants and cooperative agreements were passed as part of the 1999 Omnibus Spending Bill.

Agencies may follow other policies with grants and cooperative agreements with commercial firms. The terms of the particular grant or cooperative agreement will specify respective rights of the parties. Which data rights clause is in the grant or cooperative agreement, and its specific language, should be discussed with the Grants Officer or your General Counsel.

4.10 If the grantee assigns his copyright in scientific and technical articles produced under a Government grant to a publisher, what rights does the Government have in the article?

Pursuant to Section 36 of OMB Circular A-110(a)[112], "the Federal awarding agency(ies) reserve a royalty-free, nonexclusive and irrevocable right to reproduce, publish, or otherwise use the work for Federal purposes, and to authorize others to do so." The Government's license rights attach to the articles and later assignment by the grantee to a publisher are subject to these rights.

4.11 If the contractor assigns his copyright in scientific and technical articles produced under a Government contract to a publisher, what rights does the Government have in the article?

The Government's license rights attach to "scientific and technical articles based on or containing data first produced in the performance of a contract and published in academic, technical or professional journals, symposia proceedings or similar works" (See FAR Clause 52.227.14[113] Rights in Data General as prescribed in 27.409(a)[114]). Later assignments by the contractor to a publisher are subject to these rights.

The Contractor grants to the Government, and others acting on its behalf, a paid-up, nonexclusive, irrevocable worldwide license to reproduce, prepare derivative works, distribute copies to the public, and perform publicly and display publicly, by or on behalf of the Government.

4.12 What language could be used in a copyright agreement between a contractor or grantee author and a publisher to clarify the author's right to deposit journal articles in the electronic repository of the Government agency that funded the author's research?

In 2005, the National Institutes of Health (NIH) implemented a Policy on Enhancing Public Access to Archived Publications Resulting from NIH-Funded Research[115]. The NIH Policy explicitly recognizes and upholds the principles of copyright. Authors and journals can continue to assert copyright in NIH-funded scientific publications, in accordance with current practice. The policy encourages authors to exercise their right to give NIH a copy of their final manuscript before publication. While individual copyright arrangements can take many forms, NIH encourages investigators to sign agreements that specifically allow the manuscript to be deposited with NIH for public posting on PubMed Central[116] as soon as possible after journal publication. Institutions and investigators may wish to develop particular contract terms in consultation with their own legal counsel, as appropriate. But, as an example, the kind of language that an author or institution might add to a copyright agreement includes the following:

"Journal acknowledges that Author retains the right to provide a copy of the final manuscript to NIH upon acceptance for Journal publication or thereafter, for public archiving in PubMed Central as soon as possible after publication by Journal."

5.0   USE OF COPYRIGHTED WORKS

5.1   Use of Non-Government copyrighted works in a U.S. Government work

5.1.1   Does the U.S. Government have any special rights to use copyrighted material?

No, the U.S. Government can be held liable for violation of the Copyright Laws. Congress has expressly provided that a work protected by the Copyright Laws can be infringed by the United States (28 USC § 1498(b))[117]. The exclusive action for such infringement is an action by the copyright owner against the United States in the Court of Federal Claims for the recovery of monetary damages. However, there is no contributory copyright infringement on the part of the Government because it hasn't waived sovereign immunity rights. (John C. Boyle, 200 F.3d 1369 (Fed. Cir. 2000)[118]

While the Government may rely on fair use, the use of materials by the Government is not automatically a fair use. The U.S. Department of Justice, Office of Legal Counsel, has stated in a U.S. Department of Justice opinion[119] dated April 30, 1999, that "while government reproduction of copyrighted material for governmental use would in many contexts be non-infringing because it would be a 'fair use' under 17 USC § 107, there is no 'per se' rule under which such government reproduction of copyrighted material invariably qualifies as a fair use."
Single copy reproduction of portions of a copyrighted work for use solely for official research or related purposes is ordinarily permissible. Additionally, there may be limited exceptions in the case of National Security where the public interest results in a privilege to the Government for use of the copyrighted work without the express consent of the copyright owner. (Key Maps, Inc. v. Pruitt, 470 F. Supp. 33 (S.D. Tex. 1978)) For further discussion, see "Application of the Copyright Doctrine of Fair Use to the Reproduction of Copyrighted Material for Intelligence Purposes" by Major Gary M. Bowen. The Army Lawyer (DA Pam 27-50-332), July 2000.[120]

5.1.2   Are there any copyright issues related to the use of non-government citations or abstracts in U.S. Government authored bibliographies or databases?

Individual citations are considered facts and are not protected by copyright. However, a collection of citations may have protection as a compilation. (See FAQ Section 2.1.4)

Government use of abstracts from copyrighted sources in abstracting and indexing (A&I) services or bibliographic databases should first look to any existing license agreements between the agency and the A&I service. The A&I service may have a license agreement with the publisher for use of copyrighted information for specific purposes. However, in most cases, the A&I service does not have the right to transfer this permission to subsequent users. Therefore, if abstracts are to be used in a published bibliography, it is best to seek the permission of the copyright owners.

5.1.3 Does copyrighted material lose its copyright status and protection if it becomes part of a U.S. Government work or is included in a compilation published by the Government?

No, copyrighted material contained in a U.S. Government work does not lose its copyright status and protection. The copyright status of non-government works in a compilation is not affected by the lack of copyright protection of other works in the compilation or by the fact that the U.S. Government publishes the compilation. When copyrighted materials are included in a Government work or a compilation published by the Government, a copyright notice indicating what portions of the work are protected by copyright, and identifying the copyright owner, should be included. (See Copyright Office Circular 1[121])

5.1.4 May the U.S. Government use works of foreign governments or international organizations?

Many foreign countries provide copyright protection for works of their government. However, certain types of official works of government bodies, such as statutes and court decisions, are generally not copyrighted. Many foreign governments will consider waiving copyright upon request.

International organizations, such as the United Nations and the World Bank, also hold copyright. However, many of these documents may contain waivers or waivers may be obtained upon request. Depending on the particular agreement, the U.S. Government may have additional rights based on contributing, paying or being a sponsoring member of the organization.

5.1.5 Can the Government translate a copyrighted work to which it does not hold copyright?

Translations are considered derivative works and whether the translation of the work is fair use should be evaluated based on the fair use factors provided in the Copyright Law at 17 U.S.C. § 107[122] (See FAQ Section 2.2.2).

5.2 Use by Government libraries and archives

5.2.1 Are there any special policies that apply to Government libraries and archives?

No, there are no special policies that apply to Government libraries and archives. However, under 17 USC § 108[123], all libraries and archives are provided special rights with respect to interlibrary loan, archiving and preservation.

"It is not an infringement of copyright for a library or archives, or any of its employees acting within the scope of their employment, to reproduce no more than one copy or phonorecord of a work, or to distribute such copy or phonorecord, under the conditions specified by this section, if the…

(1) reproduction or distribution is made without any purpose of direct or indirect commercial advantage;

(2) collections of the library or archives are (i) open to the public, or (ii) available not only to researchers affiliated with the library or archives or with the institution of which it is a part, but also to other persons doing research in a specialized field; and

(3) reproduction or distribution of the work includes a notice of copyright."

Specific guidelines on photocopying and interlibrary loan are also provided in the CONTU Guidelines on Photocopying under Interlibrary Loan Arrangements,[124] and in Copyright Office Circular 21: Reproductions of Copyrighted Works by Educators and Librarians.[125]

5.2.2   Can copyrighted material be copied for library archival purposes?

Section 108 of the Copyright Act[126] addresses library archiving. The Digital Millennium Copyright Act[3] amended Sec. 108 to cover both digital and non-digital copies. It permits the creation of three copies only if the library or archives has, after reasonable effort, determined that an unused replacement cannot be obtained at a reasonable price. These copies may not be distributed to the public outside the premises of the library or archive. The material may also be converted to a new format for preservation.

Although, the Sonny Bono Copyright Term Extension Act added 20 years to the term of copyright, it also added section 108(h), allowing libraries and archives to make copies of text works that were no longer being sold and copies of which cannot be obtained at a reasonable price for preservation purposes during the 20-year extension period. Title IV "Preservation of Orphan Works Act" contained in the "The Family Entertainment and Copyright Act of 2005" amends section 108(i) and 108(h) to now include musical works; pictorial, graphical and sculptural works; and most motion pictures and other audiovisual works.

5.2.3   What happens if the actual need for copyrighted material exceeds the exceptions granted in 17 USC §§ 107 and 108?

When the anticipated needs for copyrighted material exceed the exceptions granted in § 107[127] and §108[128], then the agency, library or the patron should seek permission or license agreements. Two approaches to managing these permissions and licenses are to enter into an agreement with the copyright owner directly or to establish an agreement with a copyright clearance center (see FAQ Section 6).

5.2.4   Do copyright principles apply to materials purchased and licensed by Government libraries?

Federal librarians procure published materials in a variety of formats for the use of federal employees and the public. Generally, federal libraries do not own copyrights in the materials in their collection. In the paper environment, libraries usually purchase copies to add to their collections. Copyright law, fair use, and the "first sale" doctrine address the rights and responsibilities of the library as purchaser and of its users. However, in the digital environment,

27

while copyright principles apply, the rights of the library and its users are usually negotiated through contractual agreements and licenses. The terms of these agreements usually allow viewing materials and making reasonable copies for personal or agency use, but most specifically forbid substantial or systematic reproduction and systematic supply or distribution to non-authorized users.

It is important to work with your agency contracting officer and legal advisor in negotiating license agreements for databases, e-books, electronic journals or other subscription products. For further discussion and guidance, see the FEDLINK Video Presentation *Licensing Electronic Publications for Use in a Federal Agency*,[129] CENDI's *License Agreements for Electronic Products and Services: Frequently Asked Questions*,[130] and the National Library of Medicine *Policy on Acquiring Copyrighted Material in Electronic Format*.[131] Libraries should be proactive in informing and educating users about copyright and information license agreements. For examples, see the Naval Research Laboratory Library *Use and Disclaimer Notice*[132] and Smithsonian Institution Libraries *Permissions: Using Digital Materials from the Smithsonian Institution Libraries*.[133]

5.3 Permissions, licenses and releases to use copyrighted works

5.3.1 How can you determine if copyright permission is needed?

Permission is not needed if the work is in the public domain (see FAQ Section 2.2.4), when the use is a fair use (see FAQ Section 2.2.2), or if a license or agreement covers the intended use. Otherwise, permission should be sought.

5.3.2 Is it necessary to get permission to use facts from a copyrighted source?

Permission is not needed for the use of facts, because Copyright Law does not protect facts. However, to the extent that the facts are presented in tables, chart, graphs, or figures that can be copyrighted, permission may be necessary. Although it is always desirable to give attribution to the source, attribution is not a substitute for permission.

5.3.3 What should be considered when getting a license, release or permission?

Reasonable rights should be requested, covering the uses for which the work is intended to be utilized and considering potential uses in the future. Copyright owners generally treat permissions as being more informal than licenses. Permissions are usually royalty-free, so the rights requested should be reasonably narrow. However, licenses and releases often require a royalty or one-time payment. In all cases, consideration should be given to platforms/formats, geographical or marketing areas, duration, warranties and indemnities for incorrect information, one-time only or multiple uses, and current version versus revisions.

The wording should be developed with your Office of General Counsel. However, the final product will be only as comprehensive as the information you have provided to the counsel concerning your intended use of the material.

Many publishers have examples of permissions posted. A sample letter requesting permission is available from the University of Texas.[134]

5.3.4 Are there other rights that should be addressed regarding the U.S. Government's use of non-government works?

Yes, these may include the rights of privacy and publicity. For example, a release should be sought in all cases where a person's voice or recognizable image will be included in the Government work. While a release may have been obtained for one purpose, it may not necessarily cover additional uses. If authorization to use a picture or video for government purposes is obtained, use for non-governmental purposes may require additional authorization. For example, if a picture or video is being provided to a commercial firm for commercial use, the original release may not apply. Your General Counsel should review the original release.

5.3.5 Can the Government transfer licenses or permissions?

The ability to transfer permission depends on the original agreement between the copyright owner and the party to which the permission was originally granted. Permission obtained from a copyright owner is not transferable to a third party, unless expressly stated. If a Government agency has obtained a government-wide permission, it may provide the material to other agencies.

5.3.6 Must the Government request permission to include copyrighted material owned by a government employee in a U.S. Government work?

Yes. The Government or any other entity wishing to include copyrighted materials in a publication must seek permission from any copyright owner (See FAQ Section 5.1.1). For limitations on a government employees' right to sue the Government for copyright infringement, see 28 U.S.C. § 1498(b)[135].

5.3.7 Does a government agency need a license to perform copyrighted music or show a copyrighted video at a government sponsored meeting or event?

The agency may not need a license if the event is not open to the public and less than a substantial number of persons may attend; if the performance falls within fair use; or if the performance of the copyrighted work is in the course of face-to-face teaching or is otherwise exempt under § 110[136].

This question primarily involves whether or not this is a "public performance." 17 U.S.C. § 106(4)[137] provides the copyright owner with the exclusive right to "perform the copyrighted work publicly," but this exclusive right does not extend to private performances, and the agency may show the video if the performance were considered to be private. "Public performance" means: 1) to perform or display a work at a public place or any place where a substantial number of persons (other than a family and its social circle) are gathered; or 2) to transmit or communicate a performance or display to a place specified in (1) or to the public, regardless of whether the performance or display is received in one or more places and at the same time or at different times, see 17 U.S.C. § 101[138].

With respect to a "substantial number of persons," The House Committee on the Judiciary Report to accompany S.22, which became the Copyright Act of October 1976, P.L. 94-553, 90 Stat. 2541, indicated that routine meetings of businesses and governmental personnel would be excluded because they do not represent the gathering of a "substantial number of persons." See H.R. Rep. No. 1476, 94th Cong.2d Sess. 64, reprinted in 1976 U.S. Code Cong. & Adm. News 5659, 5677-78[139].

The House Report, however, is not the law, although a court might look to it if it found the law to be ambiguous and that the Report helped explain Congress's intent concerning the ambiguity; further, the Report is arguably inconsistent with the statutory language's reference to a family and its social circle. See Patry on Copyright, §14:25[140]. Rather than relying on this statement in the House Report, all aspects of the intended use, intended audience, and location of the performance should be examined.

Neither the law nor the House Report defines a "substantial number of persons," and the House Report does not define "routine meeting." However, the fewer the number of attendees and more often the gatherings take place, the more likely a meeting is to be "routine" and to have fewer than "a substantial number" of persons. Note that the meeting is what must be routine; routine copyright violations are not permitted.

Regardless of the audience's size, events that are open to the public usually constitute a "public performance," even if the performance occurs in a private or "semipublic place," such as an office. See Columbia Pictures Industries, Inc. v. Redd Horne Inc[141], 568 F.Supp 494 (W.D.Pa. 1983) aff'd 749 F.2d 154 (3d Cir, 1984). In this case the court found it unnecessary to consider whether a substantial number of people were gathered, finding that the video booths in question were "open to the public" and citing H.R.Rep. No. 1476, 94th Cong.2d Sess. 64, "One of the principal purposes of the definition [of "publicly"] was to make clear that, contrary to the decision in Metro-Goldwyn-Mayer Distributing Corp. v. Wyatt, 21 C.O. Bull. 203 (D. Md. 1932), performances in 'semipublic' places such as clubs, lodges, factories, summer camps, and schools are 'public performances' subject to copyright control."

Notwithstanding 17 U.S.C. § 106[142], a public performance may be a "fair use" of a copyrighted work, see 17 U.S.C. § 107[143]. Whether or not a group charges an admission fee for the event is not determinative as to whether there is a copyright violation: in addition to the effect on the market for the work, the purpose of the use, nature of the work, and amount of the work (such as a video clip vs. the whole video) that is performed are also key considerations. For guidance on "fair use," see FAQ section 2.2.2.

Performance of a work by instructors or pupils in the course of face-to-face teaching activities of a nonprofit educational institution, in a classroom or similar place devoted to instruction does not infringe copyright, see 17 U.S.C. § 110(1)[144]. Non-dramatic literary or music works, such as certain nonprofit musical performances, may also be performed without permission under specific circumstances. See, e.g., § 110(4)[145].

5.4　Infringement by the Government

5.4.1　What acts constitute a copyright infringement?

Unauthorized use of a copyrighted work is an infringement unless the use is outside the exclusive rights provided by the Copyright Law, or unless the use is covered by one of the limitations on the exclusive right, such as fair use under 17 U.S.C. § 107,[146] reproduction by libraries or archives under 17 U.S.C. § 108,[147] or transfer of particular copies or phonorecords (first sale doctrine) under 17 U.S.C. §109.[148] Once the copyright is registered in the U.S. Copyright Office, the owner of the exclusive rights infringed is entitled to institute an infringement action.

5.4.2　Can a copyright owner sue the Government if the Government or a contractor performing under a government contract, infringes the copyright?

Yes. Title 28 U.S.C. § 1498(b)[149] specifies that a copyright owner's exclusive remedy shall be an action against the United States in the U.S. Court of Federal Claims. The suit must be initiated within three years of the act of infringement. The U.S. Government is also liable for infringement by a government contractor if the contractor acted with the authorization or consent of the Government. DOD agencies process administrative claims of copyright infringement in accordance with DFARS Subpart 227.70[150].

5.4.3　What are the consequences for infringement by U.S. Government agencies?

In accordance with 28 U.S.C. 1498(b)[151], the Government's liability is for either the reasonable and entire compensation or the minimum statutory damages. The minimum statutory damages are $750 per infringement. Therefore, neither willful nor innocent infringement is an issue when determining damages for the Government.

5.4.4　Who represents the government in copyright infringement suits?

The Department of Justice represents the government in court.

6.0　APPLICABLE COPYRIGHT LEGISLATION AND OTHER RESOURCES ON THE INTERNET (originally published as Bibliography on Copyright: Education and Fair Use Issues, 12/26/00, used courtesy of Mary Levering, U.S. Copyright Office)

This bibliography lists some recent publications, articles, brochures, websites, and listservs related to copyright educational and library fair use issues that provide information and a variety of perspectives on these issues. This list is not intended to be exhaustive nor does the U.S. Copyright Office necessarily endorse the work listed. Website addresses cited were all correct and active as of August 2004.

U.S. Copyright Office Sources

U.S. Copyright Office. *Copyright Act of 1976*, as amended.
　　　　<http://www.copyright.gov/title17/92chap1.html> [U.S. Copyright Law. 17 U.S.C. §§ 101, et seq.]

U.S. Copyright Office. *Copyright Basics.* Circular 1, 1996. 12 pp.
<http://www.copyright.gov/circs/circ1.html> [Copyright Office Circular 1 provides general information and answers some basic questions that are frequently asked about copyright.]

U.S. Copyright Office. *Fair Use*, FL 102 (form letter), December 1994. 1 p.
<http://www.copyright.gov/fls/fl102.pdf> [Form letter summarizing basic fair use principles.]

U.S. Copyright Office. *DMCA Section 104 Report*, August 2001. 166 pp. plus appendices
<http://www.copyright.gov/reports/studies/dmca/dmca_study.html>
[This Report, pursuant to § 104 of the Digital Millennium Copyright Act, describes the effects of DMCA's Title 1 and the development of electronic commerce and associated technology on the operation of 2 sections of the Copyright Act which limit exclusive rights (§ 109 "effect of transfer of particular copy or phonorecord" and § 117 "computer programs" of Title 17 U.S.C, as amended); the report evaluates the relationships between existing and emerging technology and the operation of these sections.]

U.S. Copyright Office. *Report on Copyright and Digital Distance Education*, May 1999. 170 pp. Plus appendices. <http://www.copyright.gov/disted/>
[This report gives an overview of the nature of distance education as of mid-'99, describes licensing practices in digital distance education (including problems and future trends), the status of technologies relating to delivery of distance education courses and protection of their content; discusses prior initiatives to address copyright issues through negotiation of guidelines or enactment of legislation, and analyzes the application of Copyright Law to digital distance education.]

U.S. Copyright Office. *Reproduction of Copyrighted Works by Educators and Librarians.* Circular 21, 1992. 26 pp. <http://www.copyright.gov/circs/circ21.pdf>
[This circular includes excerpts from pertinent Congressional documents and legislative provisions relating to fair use and library photocopying in the U.S. Copyright Law, and other relevant documents dealing with reproduction of copyrighted works by librarians and educators. It includes the 4 sets of educational and library fair use guidelines incorporated in U.S. congressional documents in 1976 and 1981.]

U.S. Copyright Office. *Website.* <http://www.copyright.gov>
[Most of the information published by the U.S. Copyright Office on paper is also available for viewing and downloading from the Office's website and gopher site, including information circulars, federal copyright regulations, the Register's testimony, the Office's recent major reports, application forms, and access to Copyright Office records from 1978. To access Copyright Office online databases of copyright records, use <telnet: locis.loc.gov>.]

CONFU (Conference on Fair Use, 1994-98)

U.S. Information Infrastructure Task Force, Working Group on Intellectual Property Rights, Bruce Lehman, Chair. *The Conference on Fair Use: Report to the Commissioner on the Conclusion of the Conference on Fair Use.* Washington, DC. U.S. Patent and Trademark Office. 1998. 189 pp.
<http://www.uspto.gov/web/offices/dcom/olia/confu/confurep.htm>
[The CONFU November 1998 Final Report and the September 1997 First Phase Report document the genesis and history of CONFU, contain proposals for educational fair use guidelines for distance learning (Appendix I), and for digital images (Appendix H), the guidelines adopted for educational multimedia, the uniform preamble accepted by CONFU participants (Appendix G), the "Statement on Use of Copyrighted Computer Programs (Software) in Libraries--Scenarios" (Appendix K), together with all of the individual comments and institutional notifications received concerning the proposals for guidelines and information about the participating organizations.]

Other Sources

Association of Research Libraries. *Principles For Licensing Electronic Resources.* July 15, 1997. 6 pp.
<http://www.arl.org/sc/licensing/licprinciples.shtml>
[Six library associations, representing an international membership of libraries of all types and sizes, developed this statement of principles to guide libraries in negotiating license agreements for access to electronic resources so as to create agreements that respect the rights and obligations of both parties.]

Besenjak, Cheryl. *Copyright Plain and Simple*. Franklin Lakes, NJ. Career Press, 1997. 192 pp.
[This handbook on copyright principles and procedures outlines the fundamental elements of copyright in plain and simple language and through practical examples as part of the Career Press "Plain and Simple" series.]

Bruwelheide, Janis H. and Mary Hutchings Reed. *The Copyright Primer for Librarians and Educators*. Chicago, IL: American Library Association, and Washington, DC: National Education Association, 2d edition, 1995. 160 pp.
[This resource for educators and librarians in a question-and-answer format offers commentary on critical developments, especially those related to video, digitization and emerging technology, addressing issues such as fair use, copyright and photocopying for library & educational purposes from an educator's perspective.]

Computer Science and Telecommunications Board, National Research Council. *The Digital Dilemma: Intellectual Property in The Information Age*. Washington, DC. National Academy Press, 2000. 340 pp.
<http://www.nap.edu/books/0309064996/html>
[This report by the Committee on Intellectual Property Rights in the Emerging Information Infrastructure describes the multiple facets of digitized intellectual property, defining terms, identifying key issues, and explaining alternatives, and follows the complex threads of law, business, incentives to creators, the American tradition of access to information, the international context and the nature of human behavior. NAP announcement fall 2000.]

Consortium for Educational Technology for University Systems. *Fair Use of Copyrighted Works: A Crucial Element in Educating America*. Seal Beach, CA: CSU Chancellor's Office, 1995. 34 pp. [California State University, State University of New York, City University of New York.]
<http://www.cetus.org/fairindex.html>
[A consortium of three major universities, the CSU-SUNY-CUNY Work Group on Ownership, Legal Rights of Use, and Fair Use, address copyright and fair use in the context of higher education, includes analyses of court decisions on educational fair use.]

Crews, Kenneth D. Copyright Essentials for Librarians and Educators. Chicago, IL: American Library Association, 2000. 143 pp.
[This analysis by Kenneth Crews, with contributions from Dwayne K. Butler and others, was a project of the Copyright Management Center of Indiana University - Purdue University (which is directed by Crews who serves as Associate Dean of the Faculties for Copyright Management) and is intended to help professionals that provide information to the public understand and apply copyright law, and make informed and appropriate decisions about protecting copyright when using new formats and delivery systems that make duplication and transfer of information so easy.]

Crews, Kenneth D. *Copyright Law and Graduate Research: New Media, New Rights and Your Dissertation*. Ann Arbor, MI: UMI Company, 1996. 29 pp.
[This useful manual explains the fundamentals of copyright and is intended to help university students and faculty advisors understand their legal rights and responsibilities regarding the use of others copyrighted works. It explains when to seek copyright permissions and how to obtain them and also provides guidance on how to protect one's own copyrighted works.]

Crews, Kenneth D. *Copyright, Fair Use, and the Challenge for Universities: Promoting the Progress of Higher Education*. Chicago, IL: The University of Chicago Press, 1993. 256 pp.
[An explanation of copyright and the ambiguous concepts of fair use as they affect and are affected by higher education. The first large-scale study of its kind surveys the copyright policies of 98 American research universities and reveals a variety of ways in which universities have responded to--and how they could better manage--the conflicting goals of copyright policies--avoiding infringements while promoting lawful uses that serve teaching and research. *Introduction*.]

Perspectives on ... Fair Use, Education, and Libraries: A Town Meeting to Examine the Conference on Fair Use. Lois Lunin, ed., Kenneth D. Crews and Dwayne K. Buttler, guest eds. Journal of the American Society for Information Science. Vol. 50, 1999.
[This special issue of *JASIS* Perspectives contains several articles by presenters at the 2d town meeting on fair use, "Fair Use, Education and Libraries: a Town Meeting to Explore the Conference on Fair Use", hosted by the Indiana University Institute for the Study of Intellectual Property and Education and held at the campus of Indiana University-Purdue University in Indianapolis, Indiana, on April 4, 1997.]

Fair Use Guidelines for Educational Multimedia. Nonlegislative Report of the Subcommittee on Courts and Intellectual Property, Committee on the Judiciary, U.S. House of Representatives. September 27, 1996. 12 pp.

> <http://www.ccumc.org/system/files/MMFUGuides.pdf>
> [The Consortium of College and University Media Centers coordinated development of these guidelines during 1994-96, together with numerous participating organizations in a parallel initiative to CONFU; these guidelines were completed in September 1996 and acknowledged by the U.S. Congress in this Nonlegislative Report.]

Gasaway, Laura N., editor. *Growing Pains: Adapting Copyright for Libraries, Education and Society.* Littleton, CO: Fred B. Rothman & Co., 1997. 558 pp.

> [Collection of 20 essays written by a variety of scholars with expertise in the fields of Copyright Law, education, and librarianship who advocate changes in the copyright statute, in interpretations of the law, and in school and library practices so that librarians and educators can meet their obligations.]

Gasaway, Laura N. and Sarah K. Wiant. *Libraries and Copyright: A Guide to Copyright Law in the 1990s.* Washington, DC: Special Libraries Association, 1994. 271 pp.

> [Both authors are directors of university law libraries and professors of law; this source covers the functions and uses of Copyright Law, geared primarily to librarians and anyone engaged in the lending of and dissemination of copyrighted works.]

Goldstein, Paul. *Copyright's Highway: From Gutenburg to the Celestial Jukebox.* New York, NY: Hill and Wang, 1994. 261 pp.

> [Copyright expert Paul Goldstein, Professor of Law at Stanford University, traces the 300-year old history of copyright, explains the concepts and rationale behind the idea of intellectual property rights, and highlights noteworthy legal battles, (including the famous Williams & Wilkins photocopying case). Booklist, Dec. 1, 1994.]

Hardy, I.Trotter. *Project Looking Forward: Sketching the Future of Copyright in a Networked World-Final Report.* Washington, DC: U.S. Copyright Office, May 1998. 304 pp.

> <http://www.copyright.gov/reports/thardy.pdf>
> [A report commissioned by the U.S. Copyright Office from I. Trotter Hardy, Professor of Law, College of William and Mary, as part of the U.S. Copyright Office's continuing effort to examine the future of the Internet and related digital communication's technologies, and to identify legal and policy issues that might arise as a result. Copies are available from the U.S. Government Printing Office - stock number 030-002-00191-8.]

Harper, Georgia. *Will We Need Fair Use in the Twenty-First Century?* March 4, 1997. 31 pp.

> <http://www.utsystem.edu/ogc/intellectualproperty/fair_use.htm>
> [The author, a copyright lawyer in the Office of General Counsel of the University of Texas System, explores the meaning of fair use to "focus attention on those parts of its function that are most affected by the electronic environment; an examination of that effect; an evaluation of the supposed benefits of fair use and alternative ways to achieve those benefits given the impact of the electronic environment on fair use."]

Malero, Marie C. *A Legal Primer on Managing Museum Collections.* Washington, DC: Smithsonian Institution Press, 2 ed. 1998.

> [This source has an informative 50-page discussion on copyright issues for museums, written by former Smithsonian Institution Assistant General Counsel Ildiko DeAngelis.]

Shapiro, Michael S. and Brent I. Miller. *A Museum Guide to Copyright and Trademark.* Washington, DC: American Association of Museums, 1999. 226 pp.

> [This *Museum Guide* is designed to guide informed decisions by museums about how to manage intellectual property owned by the museums and that of others that museums hold in trust, and how to establish best practices for developing institutional policy and procedural statements.]

Templeton, Brad. *10 Big Myths About Copyright Explained: An Attempt to Answer Common Myths About Copyright Seen on the Net.* <http://www.templetons.com/brad/copymyths.html>

> [This web-based essay by a publisher of an electronic newspaper on the net is an attempt to answer common "myths" about copyright seen on the Net and covers issues related to copyright and Usenet/Internet publication.]

Websites (with Copyright Information)

These websites contain references, inks, and additional informational resources and opinions on copyright, educational and library fair use issues. Many of these sites have links to other informational materials with related copyright themes.

Fair Use Guidelines for Educational Multimedia. <http://www.ccumc.org/copyright/ccguides html>
> [Development of these fair use guidelines was coordinated by the Consortium of College and University Media Centers during 1994-96, together with numerous participating organizations. The guidelines were recognized by the U.S. Congress in a Nonlegislative Report dated September 27, 1996.]

Indiana University. Copyright Management Center. <http://www.copyright.iupui.edu/ >[Maintained as a resource for the academic community, this site offers access to resources about copyright and its importance to higher education. Topics of particular interest include fair use and distance learning.]

Library of Congress. *American Memory: How to Understand Copyright Restrictions.*
> <http://memory.loc.gov/ammem/ndlpedu/start/cpyrt/index html>
> [The Library of Congress provides general information on copyright, fair use and questions related to classroom examples from teachers, using American Memory collections, digitized by the Library of Congress and available on the Library's website.]

Music Library Association. < http://www.lib.jmu.edu/org/mla/ >
> [MLA's website on copyright, "Copyright for Music Librarians ".]

Software and Information Industry Association. <http://www.siia net>
> [SIIA, a trade association of the information industry, software developers and producers, conducts a comprehensive program of education, legal enforcement and public policy to fight the problem of software piracy; its education program provides tools for educators and others to help teach respect for copyright in software.]

Stanford University. <http://fairuse.stanford.edu/> <http://palimpsest.stanford.edu/bytopic/intprop/>
> [Websites on "Copyright and Fair Use" and "Copyright and Intellectual Property" with many documents and links related to libraries, education, copyright and fair use.]

University of Texas System. "Copyright Management Center Website."
> <http://www.utsystem.edu/OGC/intellectualproperty/cprtindx htm>
> [Contains many resources related to copyright in libraries and includes an interactive "Software and Database License Agreement Checklist."]

Washington State University. <http://publishing.wsu.edu/copyright/index html>
> [Website for the University's Copyright Office with links to articles, fact sheets and guidelines on copyright.]

When Works Pass Into the Public Domain. <http://www.unc.edu/~unclng/public-d.htm>
> [This chart, compiled by Laura N. Gasaway, outlines the duration of copyright for works covered by U.S. Copyright Law.]

Yale University. <http://www.library.yale.edu/~okerson/copyproj html>
> [Website with "Copyright Resources Online".]

Websites (for copyright licensing and permissions)

The following are some of the organizations that manage rights on behalf of rights holders and provide copyright licensing and permissions services. Others provide helpful information determining public domain works of for locating rights holders.

Art Museum Image Consortium (AMICO) <http://www.amico.org/home.html>
[AMICO is a not-for-profit association of institutions with collections of art that have come together to enable educational use of the digital documentation in their collections through licensing educational access to museum multimedia documentation.]

Authors Registry. <http://www.authorsregistry.org/>
[The Authors Registry is a non-exclusive licensor of author or agent-controlled rights including electronic and photocopy reproduction rights.]

Christian Copyright Licensing International (CCLI). <http://www.ccli.com>
[CCLI serves more than 140,000 churches worldwide to educate churches about Copyright Laws and provide licensing services for reproduction of church-related materials.]

Copyright Clearance Center (CCC). <http://www.copyright.com/ccc/viewPage.do?pageCode=cr10-n>
[The CCC is a not-for-profit organization created in 1978 at the suggestion of the U.S. Congress to help organizations and individuals comply with U.S. Copyright Law through its licensing programs which provide authorized users with a lawful means for making photocopies from its repertory of over 1,750,000 titles.]

Creative Eye. <http://creativeeyecoop.com>
[Creative Eye, a cooperative of independent photographers and illustrators, provides licensing services for images in digital form on behalf of its members through its stock agency, Mira.]

Graphic Artists Guild (GAG). <http://www.gag.org/>
[The GAG provides online portfolios of GAG members for permissions and licensing purposes]

Motion Picture Licensing Corporation (MPLC). <http://www.mplc.com>
(MPLC is a copyright licensing service authorized by major Hollywood motion picture studios and independent producers to grant "umbrella" licenses to non-profit groups businesses and government organizations for public performances of home videocassettes and videodiscs.]

Music performing rights licensing organizations.
ASCAP <http://www.ascap.com/licensing/about.html>
BMI <http://www.bmi.com/licensing/>
SESAC <http://www.sesac.com/licensing/obtain_a_license.aspx>
[These music performing rights licensing organizations represent song writers and publishers and provide information about music licensing and copyrights.]

National Association of College Stores (NACS). <http://www.nacs.org/public/industry.asp>
[The NACS website includes copyright information, Q&A concerning copyright compliance, procedures for obtaining permission to copy, including course pack permission request forms and the guidelines for classroom copying.]

National Writers Union/Publications Rights Clearinghouse (NWU/PRC). <http://www.nwu.org>
[The Publications Rights Clearinghouse is the NWU agency that collects online royalties for freelance writers.]

National Music Publishers Association/Harry Fox Agency (HFA). <http://www.nmpa.org/aboutnmpa/hfa.asp>
[The HFA, which represents over 20,000 American music publishers, was established by the National Music Publishers Association to license musical compositions for use on records, tapes, audio-visual works, CDs and computer chips for private and commercial purposes.]

Picture Archive Council of America (PACA). <http://www.pacaoffice.org/>
[PACA is the trade association for stock photography agencies in North America with almost 100 member agencies' names, addresses and contact information listed on the Website. Image users can request a complimentary copy of the PACA membership directory by fax to the PACA Office--fax# 507-645-7066 or by email <info@pacaoffice.org>.]

Publishers' Catalogues. <http://www.lights.ca/publisher>
[A worldwide directory of publishers' web pages for licensing and other purposes.]

WATCH: Writers, Artists and Their Copyright Holders.

< http://tyler.hrc.utexas.edu/>
[The WATCH website is maintained by the Harry Ransom Humanities Research Center at the University of Texas at Austin and the University of Reading to help users locate copyright holders and to provide basic information about U.S. Copyright Law to researchers.]

XanEdu. <http://www.xanedu.com>
[XanEdu, formally Campus Custom Publishing, Inc., serves educational institutions and faculties' needs for compiling course-specific anthologies and other course materials through custom publishing services including clearing copyrights, paying royalties and securing copyright permissions where necessary. XanEdu provides custom publishing services through its content distributing agreement w/ProQuest Information and Learning which provides access to a large digital commercial archive including works of 8,000 publishers worldwide including periodicals, newspapers, out-of-print books, dissertations and scholarly collections of manuscripts.]

ListServs

CNI-COPYRIGHT ListServ. <http://www.cni.org/Hforums/cni-copyright/>
[An Internet discussion list on copyright and intellectual property related issues, with discussion among diverse contributors who may have expertise on copyright or who are seeking answers to their questions, sponsored by the Coalition for Networked Information.

LibLicense ListServ. Website and Listserv. <http://www.library.yale.edu/~llicense/index.shtml>
[Licensing Electronic Resources, an Internet discussion list on library licensing issues and electronic content licensing for academic and research libraries, sponsored by Yale Univ. Lib., Commission on Preservation & Access, and Council on Library and Information Resources; includes sample license language and commentary.]

U.S. Copyright Office NEWSNET ListServ. <http://loc.loc.gov/copyright/newsnet/>
[An electronic mailing list from the U.S. Copyright Office that sends periodic email messages, which alert subscribers to congressional and other hearings, new regulations, publications and other copyright-related subjects.]

Other Sources (from CENDI Copyright Task Group)

American Association for the Advancement of Science. *Electronic Publishing in Science: Intellectual Property Protections.*
<http://www.aaas.org/spp/sfrl/projects/epub/finalrept.html>
[This AAAS project examines intellectual property issues associated with electronic publishing in science.]

Cederqvist, Fredrik. *Copyright of Government Works: An International Survey*. New York Law School.
<http://www.nyls.edu/cmc/papers/copyrite.txt>
[Lists countries that do and do not copyright government works.]

Ebbinghouse, Carol. "Not All Laws Are Free: The Importance of the Veeck *Case*". *Searcher*, Vol. 10, No.2, Feb 2002.
<http://www.infotoday.com/searcher/feb02/ebbinghouse.htm>

Gellman, Robert. *Twin Evils: Government Copyright and Copyright-like Controls Over Government Information*. Syracuse Law Review v. 45('95) p. 999-1072. ADA394923
<http://handle.dtic.mil/100.2/ADA394923>

ICSU/CODATA Summary of Database Protection Activities.
<http://www.codata.org/data_access/summary.html>

International Standards Organization. *ISO Technical Report 21449. "Content Delivery and Rights Management - Functional Requirements for Identifiers and Descriptors for Use in the Music, Film, Video, Sound Recording, and Publishing Industries"*
<http://www.nlc-bnc.ca/iso/tc46sc9/21449.htm>

[Establishes a frame of reference for describing the nature of the business and information transactions that take place in the course of production, distribution, and rights management. It focuses specifically on the requirements of the originators, producers, distributors, registration authorities, and rights administrators involved in the development and delivery of intellectual and artistic content in an attempt to define relationships to facilitate digital rights management in an e-commerce environment.]

Library of Congress. Federal Library and Information Center Committee (FLICC). *Copyright, Electronic Works, And Federal Libraries: Maintaining Equilibrium.* 1999 FLICC Forum on Federal Information Policies: A Summary of Proceedings, March 10, 1999-Library of Congress-Washington DC.
<http://lcweb.loc.gov/flicc/forum99 html>
[See "Providing Guidance-An Agency Policy on Copyright" by John Raubitschek, Patent Counsel-Department of Commerce <http://lcweb.loc.gov/flicc/forum99 html#Raubitschek>]

Kim, Yong-Chan. *Copyright and Internet Social Claims and Government's Intervention.*
<http://www.msu.edu/user/kimyong2/copy.htm>

Levitt, David S. "Copyright Protection for U.S. Government Computer Programs", *IDEA: The Journal of Law and Technology.* 40 IDEA 225 (2000), Franklin Pierce Law Center.
<http://www.ipmall.org/hosted_resources/IDEA/40_IDEA/40-2_IDEA_225_Levitt.pdf>

Manz, Paul C., et al. **"Protecting Government Works: The Copyright Issue".** *Acquistion Review Quarterly*-Winter 2002. Defense Acquistion University, Ft. Belvoir, VA. *Paul C. Manz, Michael J. Zelenka, Raymond S. Wittig, and Sally A. Smith*
<http://www.dau mil/pubs/arq/2002arq/Manz.pdf>
[The federal government, through its employees and contractors, produces commercially valuable inventions and information every day, often without any protection of the intellectual property involved. Intellectual property protection may provide sufficient incentive to investors to commercialize by granting a measure of exclusivity for a period of time. Federal program managers and directors, as well as private sector investors, should become familiar with all available intellectual property protection, such as: copyright law, including its impact on "government works," those created by federal and contract employees; the alternatives that would permit the Government to own the copyright in "government works"; the ability to allow private sector companies to assign co-authored works; and the importance to a federal technology manager of such protection.]

Mitchell, Bradley W. *Works of the United States Government: Time to Consider Copyright Protection. Thesis.* Washington D.C. George Washington University School of Law. 2002. ADA406618
<http://handle.dtic.mil/100.2/ADA406618>
[Includes a list of foreign national policies on copyright in government works and another of the policies of the 50 U.S. States.]

Modern Language Association. *MLA Position Statements and FAQs.*
<http://www.mlanet.org/government/positions/>

Nash, Ralph C. and Rawicz, Leonard. *Intellectual Property in Government Contracts.* Fourth Edition. Vols. 1-3. Washington D.C., The George Washington University, School of Law, 1999. [Vol 1: Intellectual Property Rights; Vol 2: Technical Data Rights; Vol 3: Computer Software, Information, and Contract Remedies.]

National Research Council. Committee on Issues in the Transborder Flow of Scientific Data. *Bits of Power: Issues in Global Access to Scientific Data.* 1997.
<http://books.nap.edu/catalog/5504 html>
[Chapter 4: Data from Publicly Funded Research—The Economic Perspective.
Chapter 5: The Trend Toward Strengthened Intellectual Property Rights: A Potential Threat to Public-Good Uses of Scientific Data]

National Research Council. Office of International Affairs. *Global Dimensions of Intellectual Property Rights in Science and Technology. 1993.*
<http://www.nap.edu/books/0309048338/html/index html>

National Research Council. Commission on Physical Sciences, Mathematics and Applications. *Proceedings of the Workshop on Promoting Access to Scientific and Technical Data for the Public Interest: An Assessment of Policy Options.* 1999.
<http://www.nap.edu/books/NI000903/html/>

National Research Council. Commission on Physical Sciences, Mathematics and Application. *A Question of Balance: Private Rights and the Public Interest in Scientific and Technical Databases.* 1999.
<http://www.nap.edu/books/0309068258/html/>

Nimmer, Melville B. and David Nimmer. *Nimmer on Copyright.* 5 vols. New York: Matthew Bender, 1992 (with periodic supplements).

Ockerbloom, John Mark, Editor. *The Online Books Page: Copyright and Related Issues.*
<http://digital.library.upenn.edu/books/okbooks.html#whatpd>
[Sections address public domain, permissions, and duration of copyright in the U.S. and abroad]

> *How do I find out whether the book is in the public domain?*
> <http://digital.library.upenn.edu/books/okbooks html#whatpd>
>
> *A Possible Exception for the Pre-1923 Public Domain Rule*
> <http://digital.library.upenn.edu/books/c-fineprint.html>

Okerson, Ann. *Who Owns Digital Works?: Computer Networks Challenge Copyright Law, But Some Proposed Cures May Be as Bad as the Disease.* Scientific American
<http://www.library.yale.edu/~okerson/sciam html>

Price, Brian R. *Copyright in Government Publications: Historical Background, Judicial Interpretation, and Legislative Clarification.* Military Law Review, Vol. 74: 19-65, Fall 1976. ADA392794
< http://handle.dtic mil/100.2/ADA392794>

Tresansky, John O. *Copyright in Government Employee Authored Works.* 30 Catholic Law Revue. 605 (1981). ADA392914
<http://handle.dtic mil/100.2/**ADA392914**>

United Nations Educational, Scientific and Cultural Organization (UNESCO). *Copyright Laws and Treaties of the World*, 28th Supplement. Washington DC., BNA, Inc. 2000.
[Intellectual property laws of 200 countries and 16 international conventions.]
See also National Copyright Legislation<http://www.unesco.org/culture/copy/>

U.S. National Commission on Libraries and Information Science. *Comprehensive Assessment of Public Information Dissemination June 2000* - March 2001
<http://www.nclis.gov/govt/assess/assess html>

U.S. National Commission on Libraries and Information Science. *Report on the Assessment of Electronic Government Information Products. Commissioned by the U.S. Government Printing Office, Superintendent of Documents. March 30, 1999. Executive Summary -- Key Findings.*
[Product Characteristics. 10. Fifteen percent of the products surveyed are not in the public domain, for all or part of the product (table 27, p. 45). In addition, user fees are charged for 30 percent of the products (table 24, p. 43).]
<http://www.access.gpo.gov/su docs/nclisassessment/report.html>

Government Agency Policies–A Sampling

Congressional Budget Office. *Privacy, Copyright, and Use Policies for this Web site.*
<http://www.cbo.gov/Privacy.shtml>

Government Printing Office. *Public Domain / Copyright Notic.*
<http://www.gpoaccess.gov/about/legal.html>

Library of Congress. *Legal Notices: About Copyright and Collections.*
<http://www.loc.gov/homepage/legal.html>

National Air and Space Administration (NASA). Scientific and Technical Information. *NASA Privacy and Copyright Notice.*
<http://www.sti.nasa.gov/disclaimer.html>

> *Documentation, Approval, and Dissemination of NASA Scientific and Technical Information* (NPG 2200.2A, September 3, 1997).
> <http://www.sti.nasa.gov/npghome3.htm>
>
> NPR 2200.2A *Requirements for Documentation, Approval, and Dissemination of NASA Scientific and Technical Information (STI)* w/Change 1 (9/10/03)
> <http://nodis3.gsfc.nasa.gov/displayDir.cfm?Internal_ID=N_PR_2200_002A_&page_name=main>
>
> *Restricted Distribution Types: Copyright*
> <http://publishing.grc.nasa.gov/techinfo/restrict.htm>

National Archives and Records Agency (NARA) *Terms and Conditions for Using Our Web Site. Copyright, Restrictions, and Permissions Notice*
<http://www.archives.gov/global_pages/privacy_and_use.html>

National Science Foundation. *Guidelines for Reproducing or Using Graphics from the NSF Web Site.*
<http://www.nsf.gov/home/pubinfo/reuse.htm>

U.S. Department of Agriculture

> *152.1-ARS. Procedures for Publishing Manuscripts and Abstracts with Non-USDA Publishers (Outside Publishing)* March 10, 1998
> <http://www.afm.ars.usda.gov/ppweb/152-01.pdf>
>
> National Agriculture Library (NAL). *NAL Copyright Statement.*
> <http://riley.nal.usda.gov/nal_display/index.php?info_center=8&tax_level=1&tax_subject=489#NAL%20Copyright%20Statement>

U.S. Department of Commerce

> Department of Commerce. *Administrative Order DAO 219-1: Public Communications*
> <http://204.193.232.34/cgi-bin/doit.cgi?204:112:d27ddcc65cae3134b8bf1b865dbd576aae631885580a96f24b4e675af66a10fb:267>
>
> National Institute of Standards and Technology (NIST). *Disclaimer. Use of NIST Information.*
> <http://www.nist.gov/public_affairs/disclaim.htm>

U.S. Department of Defense

> Office of the Assistant Secretary of Defense (Public Affairs). *Defenselink: DoD Webmasters Policies And Guidelines.*

<http://www.defenselink.mil/webmasters/>

Defense Information Systems Agency. (DISA) Defense Technical Information Center. *DTIC Scientific & Technical Documents Selection Criteria: Copyright.* <http://www.dtic.mil/dtic/submitting/selec_criteria.html#Copyright>

DTIC Guidelines for Determining Copyright. <http://www.dtic.mil/dtic/submitting/copyright.html>

Office of the Under Secretary of Defense (Acquisitions & Technology). Office of Acquisition Initiatives. *Intellectual Property: Navigating Through Commercial Waters (Version 1.1), October 2001.* < http://www.acq.osd.mil/dpap/Docs/intelprop.pdf>

Office of the Assistant Secretary of Defense (Command, Control, Communications & Intelligence*) WEB SITE ADMINISTRATION. Part II –Process and Procedures. November 25, 1998. INFORMATION POSTING PROCESS 3.5 Content Review 3.5.5. Copyrighted Material.* Copyrighted material will be used only when allowed by prevailing copyright laws and may be used only if the materials relate to the Component's mission. Consult with Counsel when using any copyrighted material. <http://www.defenselink.mil/webmasters/policy/dod_web_policy_12071998_with_amendments_and_corrections.html#part2>

U.S. Air Force Museum. *Privacy, Security and Use Notice.* <http://www.nationalmuseum.af.mil/main/disclaimer.asp>

U.S. Army. Army Regulation 25-30. 2 June 2004. *The Army Publishing and Printing Program.* See *Chapter 2: Publications, Section I: Statutory Restrictions and Official Publications* and *Section V: Copyright.* <http://www.usapa.army.mil/pdffiles/r25_30.pdf>

U.S. Navy. Secretary of the Navy. *SECNAV Instruction 5720.47. 1 July 1999. Policy for the Content of Publicly Accessible World Wide Web Sites.* DON Website Administration. Paragraph 3 Content (d) Specific Website restrictions (5): Web sites must not contain any material that is copyrighted or under trademark without the specific, written permission of the copyright or trademark holder. Further, the material must relate directly to the command's primary mission. Works prepared by DON personnel as part of their official duties and posted to the command Web site may not be copyrighted, nor may the Web site itself be copyrighted.

U.S. Department of Education.

ERIC Database Use Policy <http://www.eric.ed.gov/ERICWebPortal/resources/html/help/help_popup_privacy.html>

U.S. Department of Energy

Energy Information Administration. *Copyright Information.* <http://www.eia.doe.gov/neic/aboutEIA/copy_right.html>

Fermilab. DOE *Disclaimers and Copyright Notices.* <http://www.fnal.gov/pub/disclaim.html>

Fermilab. Information Resources. Department. *Policy for Execution of Copyright Transfer and Agreement Forms*

41

<http://bss.fnal.gov/techpubs/copyrtinfo.html>

Lawrence Livermore National Laboratory (LLNL). *Notice to Users. Copyright Status.*
<http://www.llnl.gov/disclaimer.html>

Los Alamos National Laboratory (LANL). *Copyright Notice for Scientific and Technical Information Only.*
<http://www.lanl.gov/misc/copyright.html>

Office of Scientific and Technical Information (OSTI). *Technical Information Management Program (TIMP)*
<http://www.osti.gov/timp.html>

U.S. Department of Health and Human Services.

Agency for Healthcare Research and Quality. *Guideline User Policies for Electronic Versions. Copyright.*
<http://www.ahcpr.gov/news/gdluser.htm#copyright>

Federal Drug Administration (FDA). *Linking To or Copying Information On the FDA Website*
<http://www.fda.gov/copyright.html>

National Institutes of Health Library. *Disclaimers - Copyright Restrictions Applicable to NIH Staff*
[http://nihlibrary.nih.gov/Disclaimers.htm]

National Library of Medicine (NLM) *Copyright Information.*
[http://www.nlm.nih.gov/copyright.html]

National Library of Medicine. (NLM) *Policy on Acquiring Copyrighted Material in Electronic Format.* April 27, 2000.
<http://www.nlm.nih.gov/pubs/acqcopyrightmat.html>

National Library of Medicine (NLM). *Agreement for the Use of Images from Visible Human Data Set.*
<http://www.nlm.nih.gov/research/visible/vhpagree.txt>

National Library of Medicine (NLM). *License Agreement for Use of the UMLS® Metathesaurus®*
<http://www.nlm.nih.gov/research/umls/license.html>

National Library of Medicine (NLM). *Fact Sheet: National Library of Medicine Trademarks.*
<http://www.nlm.nih.gov/pubs/factsheets/trademarks.html>

National Library of Medicine (NLM). *Profiles in Science FAQ 5. May I have permission to use the documents (letters, articles, photographs, etc.) from Profiles in Science?*
<http://profiles.nlm.nih.gov/Help/FAQ/#permission>

U.S. Department of Interior

U.S. Geological Survey. (USGS) *USGS Privacy Policy and Disclaimers. Copyright.*
<http://www.usgs.gov/privacy html#copyright>

U.S. Department of Justice. Computer Crime & Intellectual Property Section, Criminal Division

Federal Prosecution of Violations of Intellectual Property Rights (Copyrights, Trademarks and Trade Secrets). May 1997. Washington, D.C.
<http://www.usdoj.gov/criminal/cybercrime/CFAleghist.htm>

DOJ Criminal Resource Manual. 1854 Copyright Infringement -- First Sale Doctrine.
<http://www.usdoj.gov:80/usao/eousa/foia reading room/usam/title9/crm01854.htm>

Protecting Intellectual Property Rights: Copyrights, Trademarks and Trade Secrets
<http://www.usdoj.gov:80/criminal/cybercrime/ip html>

www.cybercrime.gov
<http://www.usdoj.gov:80/criminal/cybercrime/index html>

Copyrighted Materials and the FOIA, FOIA Update, Vol. IV, No. 4, Fall 1983, OIP Guidance
<http://www.usdoj.gov:80/oip/foia updates/Vol IV 4/page3 htm>
[In sum, agencies should carefully examine all copyrighted materials encompassed within FOIA requests to determine whether they qualify for Exemption 4 protection. As for those copyrighted materials to which Exemption 4 is inapplicable, the position of the Department of Justice is that the release of such materials under the FOIA is a defensible "fair use."]

Memorandum for Andrew J. Pincus, General Counsel, Department of Commerce From Randolph D. Moss, Acting Assistant Attorney *Opinion: RE: Whether Government Reproduction of Copyrighted Materials Invariably is a "Fair Use" under Section 107 of the Copyright Act of 1976.* April 30, 1999.
<http://lcweb.loc.gov/flicc/gc/fairuse.html>

U.S. Mint. *Privacy Policy & Terms of Use. Intellectual Property.*
<http://www.usmint.gov/policy/index.cfm?action=TermsOfUse>

U.S. Patent & Trademark Office (USPTO). *Editorial Standards Copyright and Trademark Issues RE: Materials from USPTO Website*
<http://www.uspto.gov/main/ccpubguide htm>
U.S. Patent & Trademark Office

U.S. Senate. *Photo Collection of the Senate Historical Office: Copyright Information for the Collection*
<http://www.senate.gov/artandhistory/history/common/generic/Photo Collection of the Senate Historical Office htm>

Publisher Copyright Transfer Agreements–A Sampling

Academic Press. Copyright Transfer Agreement.
<http://www.academicpress.com/www/journal/copyright htm>

American Association for Artificial Intelligence. AAAI Press Copyright Form
<http://www.aaai.org/Press/Author/copyrightform.pdf >

American Geophysical Union. Copyright Agreement
<http://www.agu.org/pubs/Copyrght.pdf>

American Physical Society. Transfer of Copyright Agreement.

<http://forms.aps.org/author/copytrnsfr.pdf>

Association for Computing Machinery. ACM Copyright Form
<http://www.acm.org/pubs/copyright_form.html>

Elsevier Author Gateway.
<http://authors.elsevier.com/>
Note: Under Publisher Information, choose Getting Published with Elsevier Science. Under After Acceptance, choose Copyright Information. Elsevier does not post its Copyright Transfer Agreement nor does the information presented on the Author Gateway mention Government or Government-contracted works.

IEEE Computer Society. Copyright Form Information.
<http://www.ieee.org/web/publications/rights/cfrmlink.html>

IEEE Copyright Form
<http://www.ieee.org/portal/index.jsp?pageID=corp_level1&path=about/documentation/copyright&file=cfrmlink.xml&xsl=generic.xsl>

BioMedical Library Association. BMLA. Notice to Authors
<http://www.mlanet.org/publications/jmla/jmlainfo.html#note>

Materials Research Society. Instructions for Authors. Copyright Transfer.
<http://www.mrs.org/publications/books/manuscript_info/proc_copyright_info.pdf>

Science Publishers
<http://www.sciencekomm.at/publish.html>

References

[1] Berne Convention http://www.copyright.gov/title17/92appii html

[2] 17 USC § 106. http://www.copyright.gov/title17/92chap1.html#106

[3] Digital Millennium Copyright Act http://www.copyright.gov/legislation/dmca.pdf

[4] 17 USC § 1202(c) http://www.copyright.gov/title17/92chap12 html#1202

[5] 17 USC § 107 http://www.copyright.gov/title17/92chap1 html#107

[6] Federal Acquisition Regulation http://www.arnet.gov/far/

[7] 17 USC § 202 http://www.copyright.gov/title17/92chap2 html#202

[8] 17 USC § 109 http://www.copyright.gov/title17/92chap1 html#109

[9] OMB Circular A-130 http://www.whitehouse.gov/omb/circulars/a130/a130trans4.html

[10] Freedom of Information Act http://www.usdoj.gov/oip/foi-act.htm

[11] Privacy Act http://www.accessreports.com/statutes/PA.htm

[12] 44 U.S.C. § 1901 http://frwebgate.access.gpo.gov/cgi-bin/getdoc.cgi?dbname=browse_usc&docid=Cite:+44USC1901

[13] 44 U.S.C. § 3301 http://frwebgate.access.gpo.gov/cgi-bin/getdoc.cgi?dbname=browse_usc&docid=Cite:+44USC3301

[14] 17 USC § 101, Definitions http://www.copyright.gov/title17/92chap1 html#101

[15] 17 USC § 101, Definitions http://www.copyright.gov/title17/92chap1 html#101

[16] 17 USC § 201(a) http://www.copyright.gov/title17/92chap2.html#201

[17] License Agreement for Use of UMLS Products http://www.nlm nih.gov/research/umls/license html

[18] 17 USC § 101, Definitions http://www.copyright.gov/title17/92chap1 html#101

[19] 17 USC § 201(d) http://www.copyright.gov/title17/92chap2 html#201

[20] 17 USC § 204 http://www.copyright.gov/title17/92chap2.html#204

[21] Title 17 of the United States Code (17 USC – Copyrights) http://www.copyright.gov/title17

[22] 37 CFR, Chapter II http://www.access.gpo.gov/nara/cfr/waisidx_99/37cfrv1_99.html

[23] U.S. Constitution, Article 1, Section 8 http://www.archives.gov/exhibits/charters/constitution_transcript.html

[24] Berne Convention http://www.copyright.gov/title17/92appii html

[25] Sonny Bono Copyright Term Extension Act http://www.copyright.gov/legislation/s505.pdf

[26] Digital Millennium Copyright Act http://www.copyright.gov/legislation/hr2281.pdf

[27] 17 USC § 106 http://www.copyright.gov/title17/92chap1.html#106

[28] 17 USC § 106a http://www.copyright.gov/title17/92chap1 html#106a

[29] Circular 101: Copyright Basics http://www.copyright.gov/circs/circ1 html

[30] Circular 40, Copyright Registration for Works of the Visual Arts http://www.copyright.gov/circs/circ40 html

[31] The U.S. Copyright Law, Chapter 3 -- Duration of Copyright http://www.copyright.gov/title17/92chap3.html

[32] Information Circular 15a - Duration of Copyright: Provisions of the Law Dealing with the Length of Copyright Protection http://www.copyright.gov/circs/circ15a.pdf

[33] Fact sheet FL 15 - New Terms for Copyright Protection http://www.copyright.gov/fls/sl15.html

[34] When Works Pass Into the Public Domain http://www.unc.edu/~unclng/public-d.htm

[34a] Copyright Term and the Public Domain in the United States http://www.copyright.cornell.edu/training/Hirtle_Public_Domain.htm

[35] 17 USC §§ 107 through 120 http://www.copyright.gov/title17/92chap1.html

[36] 17 USC § 107 http://www.copyright.gov/title17/92chap1.html#107

[37] 17 USC § 107 http://www.copyright.gov/title17/92chap1.html#107

[38] National Library of Medicine http://www nlm nih.gov/copyright html

[39] NASA Center for AeroSpace Information (CASI) http://www.sti.nasa.gov/disclaimer html

[40] Library of Congress http://www.loc.gov/homepage/legal.html#copyright

[41] 17 USC § 204 http://www.copyright.gov/title17/92chap2.html#204

[42] Copyright Office Circular 22 http://www.copyright.gov/circs/circ22.html

[43] Library of Congress Information System http://www.loc.gov/catalog/locisint.htm

[44] Washington Post http://www.washingtonpost.com/wp-srv/interact/longterm/talk/copy htm

[45] New York Times http://www nytimes.com/ref/membercenter/help/linkingfaq.html

[46] Pub. L. No 105-304, 112 Stat. 2860 http://www.copyright.gov/legislation/hr2281.pdf

[47] 17 U.S.C § 1201 et al http://www.copyright.gov/title17/92chap12 html

48 17 U.S.C. § 1201(a)(1) http://www.copyright.gov/title17/92chap12 html#1201
49 17 U.S.C. § 1201(a)(1) http://www.copyright.gov/title17/92chap12 html#1201
50 17 U.S.C. § 1202 http://www.copyright.gov/title17/92chap12 html#1201
51 17 U.S.C. § 512 http://www.copyright.gov/title17/92chap5 html#512
52 U.S. Copyright Office Summary of the DMCA. http://www.copyright.gov/legislation/dmca.pdf
53 Patents http://www.uspto.gov/web/offices/pac/doc/general/whatis htm
54 Trademarks http://www.uspto.gov/web/offices/tac/tmfaq htm#
55 U.S. Patent and Trademark Office http://www.uspto.gov/
56 17 USC § 101, Definitions http://www.copyright.gov/title17/92chap1.html#101
57 Copyright in Government Employee Authored Works http://handle.dtic.mil/100.2/ADA392914
58 Public Affairs Associate V. Rickover
http://caselaw.lp.findlaw.com/scripts/getcase.pl?court=US&vol=369&invol=111
59 17 USC § 105 http://www.copyright.gov/title17/92chap1 html#105
60 17 USC § 105 http://www.copyright.gov/title17/92chap1 html
61 Gellman http://handle.dtic.mil/100.2/ADA394923
62 Pfeiffer v. Central Intelligence Agency http://www.ll.georgetown.edu/federal/judicial/dc/opinions/94opinions/94-5107a html
63 OMB Circular A-130 http://www.whitehouse.gov/omb/circulars/a130/a130trans4.html
64 Department of Defense Directive 5230.9 http://stinet.dtic mil/stinfo/data/DoDD_52309.pdf
65 DOD Instruction 5230.29 http://www.dtic.mil/whs/directives/corres/pdf/523029p.pdf
66 Freedom of Information Act (FOIA) Exemptions http://www.usdoj.gov/oip/foi-act.htm
67 CRADA http://www.usbr.gov/research/tech-transfer/together/crada/whatcrada.html
68 NASA Space Act Agreements http://www hq.nasa.gov/ogc/samanual html
69 Terms and Conditions for the Visible Human Project http://www nlm.nih.gov/research/visible/vhpagree.txt
70 License Agreement for Use of the UMLS® Metathesaurus®
http://wwwcf.nlm.nih.gov/umlslicense/snomed/license.cfm
71 17 USC § 105 http://www.copyright.gov/title17/92chap1 html#105
72 17 USC § 403 http://www.copyright.gov/title17/92chap4.html#403
73 Matthew Bender & Co. v. West Publishing Co. http://www.law.cornell.edu/copyright/cases/158_F3d_674 htm
74 IEEE Copyright Form
http://www.ieee.org/portal/cms_docs_iportals/iportals/publications/rights/IEEECopyrightForm.pdf
75 Kluwer Academic/Plenum Publishing Transfer of Copyright Form http://www.bga.org/journal/Kluwer-Plenum_copyright.pdf
76 17 USC § 101, Definitions http://www.copyright.gov/title17/92chap1.html#101
77 17 USC § 201 http://www.copyright.gov/title17/92chap2 html#201
78 Federal Acquisition Regulations http://www.arnet.gov/far/
79 FAR Subpart 27.4—Rights in Data and Copyrights http://www.arnet.gov/far/current/html/Subpart%27_4.html
80 FAR general data rights clause, 52.227-14 http://www.arnet.gov/far/current/html/52.227 html#1109286
81 Defense Federal Acquisition Regulation Supplement (DFARS) Subpart 227.71
http://www.acq.osd.mil/dpap/dars/dfars/html/current/227_71.htm
82 Part 211 http://www.acq.osd mil/dpap/dars/dfars/html/current/211_0.htm
83 DFARS Part 252 http://www.acq.osd.mil/dpap/dars/dfars/html/current/252_1 htm
84 DFARS Part 227.72 http://www.acq.osd mil/dpap/dars/dfars/html/current/227_72.htm
85 FAR 27.400 http://www.arnet.gov/far/current/html/Subpart_27_4 html#999113
86 DFARS 227.7103-9 http://www.acq.osd mil/dpap/dars/dfars/html/current/227_71.htm#227.7103-9
87 DFARS 252.227-7013- http://www.acq.osd mil/dp/dars/dfars/html/r20030430/252227.htm#252.227-7013
88 DFARS 252.227-7020 http://www.acq.osd mil/dpap/dars/dfars/html/current/252227.htm#252.227-7020
89 FAR 27.227-20 http://farsite hill.af mil/reghtml/regs/far2afmcfars/fardfars/far/52_227.htm#P495_117738
90 DFARS 227.7103-9 http://www.acq.osd mil/dp/dars/dfars/html/r20030430/227_71.htm#227.7103-9
91 DFARS 227.7203-9 http://www.acq.osd mil/dp/dars/dfars/html/r20030430/227_72.htm#227.7203-9
92 FAR 52.227-14 http://farsite hill.af mil/reghtml/regs/far2afmcfars/fardfars/far/52_227 htm#P328_81380
93 FAR 27.404(f)(2) http://www.arnet.gov/far/current/html/Subpart%2027_4.html
94 DFARS 227.7103-9(a)(2) http://www.acq.osd.mil/dpap/dars/dfars/html/current/227_71.htm#227.7103-9
95 FAR special works data rights clause, 52.227-17

http://farsite hill.af mil/reghtml/regs/far2afmcfars/fardfars/far/52_227 htm#P444_107388

[96] FAR 27.404(g)(3) http://www.arnet.gov/far/current/html/Subpart 27_4 html

[97] NASA FAR Supplement http://www hq.nasa.gov/office/procurement/regs/5227 htm

[98] DFARS 252.227-7020 http://www.acq.osd mil/dpap/dars/dfars/html/current/252227.htm#252.227-7020

[99] FAR general data rights clause, 52.227-14 http://www.acqnet.gov/far/current/html/52_227.html

[100] FAR 27.404(g) http://www.acqnet.gov/far/current/html/Subpart%2027_4.html#wp1041836%20

[101] FAR special works data rights clause, 52.227-14(d) http://www.acqnet.gov/far/current/html/52_227.html

[102] FAR special works data rights clause http://www.acqnet.gov/far/current/html/52_227.html

[103] DFARS clause 252.227-7013 http://www.acq.osd.mil/dpap/dars/dfars/html/current/252227.htm#252.227-7013

[104] DFARS clause 252.227-7020 http://www.acq.osd.mil/dpap/dars/dfars/html/current/252227 htm#252.227-7020

[105] DFARS 227.7106(b) http://www.acq.osd.mil/dpap/dars/dfars/html/current/227_71 htm#227.7106

[106] FAR 27.404(f)(1)(v) http://farsite.hill.af.mil/reghtml/regs/far2afmcfars/fardfars/far/27.htm#P326_97762

[107] DFARS clause 252.227-7013(f) http://www.acq.osd.mil/dpap/dars/dfars/html/current/252227 htm#252.227-7013 and 252.227-7014(f) http://www.acq.osd.mil/dpap/dars/dfars/html/current/252227 htm#252.227-7014

[108] OMB Circular A-110 Uniform Administrative Requirements for Grants and Agreements With Institutions of Higher Education, Hospitals, and Other Non-Profit Organizations http://www.whitehouse.gov/omb/circulars/a110/a110 html

[109] OMB Circular A-102, Grants and Cooperative Agreements with State and Local Governments http://www.whitehouse.gov/omb/circulars/a102/a102 html

[110] Section 36 of Circular A-110 http://www.whitehouse.gov/omb/circulars/a110/a110 html#36

[111] new requirements for providing government access http://www.whitehouse.gov/omb/fedreg/a110-finalnotice html

[112] Section 36 of OMB Circular A-110(a) http://www.whitehouse.gov/omb/circulars/a110/a110.html#36

[113] FAR Clause 52.227.14 http://farsite hill.af mil/reghtml/regs/far2afmcfars/fardfars/far/52_227.htm#P248_51622

[114] 27.409(a) http://farsite.hill.af.mil/reghtml/regs/far2afmcfars/fardfars/far/27.htm#P420_100140

[115] Policy on Enhancing Public Access to Archived Publications Resulting from NIH-Funded Research http://publicaccess.nih.gov/

[116] PubMed Central http://www.pubmedcentral nih.gov/

[117] 28 USC § 1498 (b) http://www4.law.cornell.edu/uscode/html/uscode28/usc_sec_28_00001498----000- html

[118] John C. Boyle v. United States http://www.ll.georgetown.edu/federal/judicial/fed/opinions/99opinions/99-5125.html

[119] U.S. Department of Justice opinion http://lcweb.loc.gov/flicc/gc/fairuse.html

[120] "Application of the Copyright Doctrine of Fair Use to the Reproduction of Copyrighted Material for Intelligence Purposes" http://handle.dtic.mil/100.2/ADA389801

[121] Copyright Office Circular 1 http://www.copyright.gov/circs/circ1.html

[122] 17 USC § 107 http://www.copyright.gov/title17/92chap1 html#107

[123] 17 USC § 108 http://www.copyright.gov/title17/92chap1 html#108

[124] CONTU Guidelines on Photocopying under Interlibrary Loan Arrangements http://www.cni.org/docs/infopols/CONTU.html

[125] Copyright Office Circular 21 http://www.copyright.gov/circs/circ21.pdf

[126] 17 USC § 108 http://www.copyright.gov/title17/92chap1.html#108

[127] 17 USC § 107 http://www.copyright.gov/title17/92chap1 html#107

[128] 17 USC § 108 http://www.copyright.gov/title17/92chap1.html#108

[129] Licensing Electronic Publications for Use in a Federal Agency http://lcweb.loc.gov/flicc/video/licen/licen.html

[130] License Agreements for Electronic Products and Services: Frequently Asked Questions http://www.cendi.gov/publications/01-3lic_agree.html

[131] Policy on Acquiring Copyrighted Material in Electronic Format http://www nlm.nih.gov/pubs/acqcopyrightmat html

[132] Use and Disclaimer Notice http://library.nrl navy.mil/index.cfm?i=90

[133] Permissions: Using Digital Materials from the Smithsonian Institution Libraries http://www.sil.si.edu/permissions/

[134] sample letter requesting permission http://www.utsystem.edu:80/ogc/intellectualproperty/permmm htm

[135] 28 USC § 1498 (b) http://www4.law.cornell.edu/uscode/html/uscode28/usc_sec_28_00001498----000- html

[136] 17 USC § 110 http://www.copyright.gov/title17/92chap1.html#110

[137] 17 U.S.C. § 106(4) http://www.copyright.gov/title17/92chap1.html#106

[138] 17 USC § 101 http://www.copyright.gov/title17/92chap1.html#101

[139] H.R. Rep. No.94-1476 http://en.wikisource.org/wiki/Copyright_Law_Revision_(House_Report_No._94-1476)/Annotated

[140] Patry, William F. Patry on Copyright. St. Paul, MN: Thomson West (Westlaw), 2008

[141] Columbia Pictures Industries, Inc. v. Redd Horne Inc
http://www.law.cornell.edu/copyright/cases/749_F2d_154 htm

[142] 17 U.S.C. § 106 http://www.copyright.gov/title17/92chap1.html#106

[143] 17 U.S.C. § 107 http://www.copyright.gov/title17/92chap1.html#107

[144] 17 U.S.C. § 110(1) http://www.copyright.gov/title17/92chap1 html#110

[145] 17 USC § 110(4) http://www.copyright.gov/title17/92chap1 html#110

[146] 17 USC § 107 http://www.copyright.gov/title17/92chap1 html#107

[147] 17 USC § 108 http://www.copyright.gov/title17/92chap1 html#108

[148] 17 USC § 109 http://www.copyright.gov/title17/92chap1 html#109

[149] 28 USC § 1498 (b) http://www4.law.cornell.edu/uscode/html/uscode28/usc_sec_28_00001498----000- html

[150] DFARS Subpart 227.70 http://www.acq.osd.mil/dpap/dars/dfars/html/current/227_70 htm

[151] 28 USC § 1498 (b) http://www4.law.cornell.edu/uscode/html/uscode28/usc_sec_28_00001498----000- html

www.ingramcontent.com/pod-product-compliance
Lightning Source LLC
Chambersburg PA
CBHW081302180526
45170CB00007B/2532

* 9 7 8 1 5 4 4 6 5 4 3 4 8 *